^{THE} Cucumber Tree

MEMORIES OF A VANCOUVER BOYHOOD

Bob Ross

For more information contact
Sandhill Book Marketing (info@sandhillbooks.com)

LIBRARY AND ARCHIVES CANADA CATALOGUING IN PUBLICATION

Ross, Bob, 1940–

  The cucumber tree : memories of a Vancouver boyhood / Bob Ross.

ISBN 978-0-9812991-0-5

  1. Ross, Bob, 1940– —Childhood and youth. 2. Vancouver (B.C.)—Social life and customs—20th century. 3. Vancouver (B.C.)—Biography. I. Title.

FC3847.26.R68A3 2009   971.1′3304092   C2009-903683-5

Book design by Gary Wilcox
Cover design by Vancouver Desktop Publishing Centre
Printed in Canada by Hignell Book Printing

Distributed by Sandhill Book Marketing, Kelowna, B.C. *www.sandhillbooks.com*

For my children,
Christy and Karen,
and
their children . . .

Contents

Life was Simple
Me, Johnny and Tommy

Best of Times

This is the story of my childhood. My purpose in writing it is to give my grandchildren insight into their past, and perhaps to give me insight into myself. This tale might also explain to my adult daughters what may have caused their father to be such an embarrassment to them during their teenage years.

I was born at the end of 1940. It was the year after Germany invaded Poland to start World War II, and a year before the Japanese attacked Pearl Harbour. While technically I preceded the baby boomers by five years, my childhood was shaped by their same influences.

My story ends in 1958, the year I graduated from high school, the year after the Russians blasted the first man-made satellite into orbit, and over a decade before the Americans put the first man on the moon.

In Vancouver, where I was born, the 1950s were a time of unprecedented prosperity. The first half of the century had experienced the suffering of two disastrous world wars and the poverty of the Great Depression. But the fifties were a time of recovery, full employment and real wealth. Families were stable, neighbourhoods were safe. There were no drugs, no crime and, in Canada, still no welfare.

The Future Looked Bright
*The courses that our lives would follow
were uniform and predictable*

These were the best of times. Probably nowhere in the world at any time has a child had better prospects of growing up to a life of happiness and security than on the west coast of Canada in the 1950s. Like all my friends, I was destined to graduate from high school with the probability of access to a college education. The courses that our lives would follow were uniform and predictable. Everyone in my university class would be able to count on immediate employment and no debt. We all expected that in short order we would get married, have kids and buy a house on the west side of town.

Mine was probably the last generation to grow up at our mother's knee. Our dads all worked and our mothers stayed home to raise the kids and run the household. We seldom went out at night — the entire family sat down to dinner together every evening, unhurried by outside commitments or TV schedules. All kids had chores, and most attended church or Sunday school.

We didn't have television. Life was simpler, its pace was slower and people had more time for each other. With no electronic gadgets, children learned by direct experience. Kids weren't smothered with supervision and organized activities. There was no paranoia about drugs or sexual predators, and children were given the freedom to explore by themselves. Without shopping malls, fast food outlets, cell-phones or internet chat rooms, most childhood explorations were in the natural, rather than the built or electronic world. Kids were therefore more attuned to nature — mankind's traditional source of direct insights.

Under these conditions, my childhood was idyllic.

But as I entered my teens, I saw a dark cloud on the horizon. I developed a gnawing anxiety about war. The 1950s were the beginning of the Cold War, and I harboured a nagging fear that the Russians would bomb Vancouver in their attempt to annihilate the capitalist empire of America. And so I became preoccupied with learning the survival skills that would allow me to escape to the northern wilderness where I could live off the land.

As it turned out, these skills were never put to the ultimate test. Of course I have no regrets about that. But I will forever cherish learning those skills, for they have enriched my entire life. And it is the adventures of our childhood that empower us to explore the world as adults.

Our Macdonald Street Home — 1940
Johnny beating a trail to the snowman

Chapter 1

Macdonald Street

The world of my childhood was Macdonald Street, which was named after Sir John A, the Father of Confederation. Mum insisted that we spell it as one word, with a full *Mac* and a small *d*, because that's how Sir John A spelled it.

Our house on Macdonald Street was between 45th and 47th Avenues (there is no 46th). Ours was one of the largest blocks of single family homes in the city, with properties of unusual size. The lots were so full of big trees that the hedges and low fences in front of each home merely added to the feel of a country road passing through a forest. The roadway was edged with gravel shoulders, and grass boulevards lined both sides. The homes were served by long driveways, and the absence of parked cars and lack of cross-streets gave the streetscape a leafy, woodland feeling.

Macdonald Street didn't carry much traffic in those days. I remember the horse carts in the 1940s delivering milk and coal and fresh vegetables up and down the street. When the horses stopped outside our house at lunch time, the delivery man attached a feedbag of oats over their noses. And the horses peed and left their turds where they stood, resting in their traces at the edge of the road. When the rains came, the turds washed away in the rivulets that formed in the gravel beside the pavement.

Everybody on Macdonald Street knew everybody else. In the first fifteen years of my life nobody moved away from Macdonald Street and nobody moved in. The fences between properties were humble and inconspicuous, and we ran back and forth through our neighbours' yards without asking permission or feeling like we were intruding. We always said "hello," or called out "have a nice day" when we saw one another. We seldom locked our doors.

Three other families on Macdonald Street had kids that I played with. The Williams boys, who lived across the street, were closest in age to my brother Johnny and me. Donald, the youngest Williams boy, was in my grade at school, and throughout our childhood we were inseparable best friends. Donald was much bigger and stronger than I, and shouldered most of the burden when we discovered new activities and adventures. In later years, whenever I was asked in aptitude tests or questionnaires who I had gone to for advice as an adolescent — father, relative, teacher, clergyman — I always answered "Donald."

One of his brothers, Paul, was a year older. Paul's childhood was defined by the many wild creatures which he kept in cages out in the woodshed. Whenever one of his creatures died, Paul performed an autopsy, which is how I learned that snakes have backbones and how to determine the sex of a rabbit. The oldest Williams boy was named John. He was five years older than me, and was very popular with the girls at school. Since his girlfriends didn't care much about dissecting dead snakes and rabbits, whenever John ran into his brothers at school he pretended he didn't know them.

Next door to the Williams, lived the Wollaston family. The Wollastons owned an exceptional property. It was full of trees, whose high branches were the meeting places for all us kids. It had a lawn big enough to be the neighbourhood football stadium. Their fish pond was our ice-hockey rink, and the driveway encircling the Wollaston's house was the circuit for many a bike race. The Wollastons had a daughter, Elsie, who was three years younger than me. She was a brain and excelled at

The Macdonald Street Gang
Pyramid bottom row: *Paul, Donald, Johnny.* Middle row: *Me, Patience.*
Top: *Jonathan* Seated behind: *Stephen* *(Elsie absent)*

school work. She didn't excel at football or hockey or bike-racing, but we had to include her in our activities because we usually did them in her yard.

Elsie's birthday was on December 31, and she always invited the neighbourhood kids to her party on New Years Eve. We'd play musical chairs and pin-the-tail-on-the-donkey and sing "Old Mac-Donald's Farm." But the highlight of her party each year was a magician who impressed me so much that I developed my own repertoire of parlour magic. Now I, too, can pass a knitting needle through an inflated balloon or chop through your finger with a blunt guillotine.

On the other side of the Wollastons, at the corner of Macdonald and 47th, lived the Silbernagel family. Their eldest kid, named Patience, was a year younger than me. She had flaming red hair and was good at climbing trees and kicking footballs. She had two brothers: Jonathan, who was a year younger, and Stephen, who had trouble keeping up because he wasn't born until I was six years old.

Another member of our neighbourhood gang was my brother Johnny, who was sixteen months older than me. Being brothers, Johnny and I played together a lot — until about the age of eight, when I

7

The Toboggan Team
Training for a run down the big Macdonald Street hill

discovered that he couldn't back up his claim that he knew everything in the world. Our bond weakened when Johnny began to realize that he couldn't climb a tree as fast, or kick a ball as straight, as his younger brother. But we played together so long as he was able to settle our disputes by sitting on my head or pinning me in half-Nelsons. By the time we entered out teens, our interests were diverging rapidly. Eventually Johnny and I saw each other only on weekends because, in his last two years of high school, he was a weekly boarder at private school.

So the Macdonald Street Gang consisted of two Williams boys, two Ross boys, Jonathan and two girls. There was a span of almost six years between Paul, who was the oldest, and Elsie, who was the youngest. I was lucky because my age was right in the middle.

I should also include our dog, Tommy, who was a Springer spaniel and an enthusiastic participant in everything we did. Tommy's specialties were pulling our sleighs and wagons, and finding baseballs that we hit over the fence into neighbours' yards. He was also very good at scaring the hell out of motorists by darting back and forth across Macdonald Street without warning.

No matter what the season, there was always some attraction that drew us together to play at the edge of Macdonald Street. On rainy days we made dams in the ditches and floated sticks and paper boats. On dark days we tormented motorists with pull-the-rope, and on many an evening we played knocky-nine-doors on the neighbours' homes.

In the autumn, when the leaves fell from the trees, we'd gather around the bonfires beside the road where the fallen leaves were raked into little piles for burning. If the leaves were damp, these roadside fires would smoulder for days, like the peat fires of Ireland. I loved scooping holes in the embers and roasting apples or potatoes stolen from a neighbour's garden, my nose twitching and eyes watering from the clouds of acrid smoke which lingered in the damp air.

I loved, too, the winter days when Macdonald Street was covered with snow. In the late 1940s and early '50s Vancouver had many heavy snowfalls. For short periods each winter, Macdonald Street became the perfect sleigh hill. And when the snow ploughs finally exposed the pavement in front of our house, we moved down the street to 49th Avenue and tobogganed down Macdonald Street where it was too steep for the ploughs. Sometimes these sleigh rides were terrifying. I remember when three or four of us were packed into a toboggan, hanging on for dear life, as we rocketed across Marine Drive at the foot of the steep hill, relying on Jonathan to stop any cars as we hurtled past on our way to the farmland below. Traffic was light in those days — you couldn't get away with that today, not with Marine Drive's daily volume of almost 30,000 vehicles.

In those days, Macdonald Street ran all the way to the Fraser River. Below Marine Drive, Macdonald's steep hill ended at the rich soil of the river delta, where farms flourished on both sides of the street. It was a mile from our house to the river, and for the kids in our neighbourhood Macdonald Street was a lifeline to a world of adventure beyond the city. Before my school years, Mum would walk us down Macdonald to the "flats" so that we could see the lambs and foals at play, or watch cows being milked, or feed apples through the fences to curious horses. It was on the flats that I received my earliest lessons about the cycles of the seasons — from the springtime chorus of frogs and song birds and the birthing of farm animals to the autumn harvests and the flocks of migrating geese.

Where Macdonald Street ran through the farmland there were deep ditches along its edges, and in their murky water Mum showed us frogs and muskrats and water birds. Later, when I was of school age, the kids of my neighbourhood returned to the flats without our mothers, coasting down Macdonald on our wagons, laden with glass jars and nets to search its ditches and sloughs for tadpoles and frogs and stickle-backs for our backyard aquariums.

Vancouver's first (and last) farm was located at the foot of Macdonald Street. It was the McCleery dairy farm, subsequently sold and redeveloped as the McCleery Golf Course in 1959. As we grew older we helped Gerry Logan, grandson of one of the original McCleery homesteaders, bring in the hay and milk his cows. In the ensuing years we often trekked down Macdonald to trap muskrats in its ditches, or snare its pheasants and shoot its ducks with our bows and arrows. And many a wintry evening I've wearily trudged up the Macdonald Street hill with my skates and hockey stick slung over my shoulder after a day of shinny in the frozen fields by the river.

In 1947, when Donald and I were in first grade at Kerrisdale School, the BC Electric Company started a new bus service which looped down Macdonald Street to 49th Avenue and back up Carnarvon Street to connect with the 41st Avenue streetcars. There was one bus driver that we kids got to know very well and, before long, riding the buses became part of our regular play.

The stopover where the bus driver rested for ten minutes on each circuit was right in front of the Silbernagels' house. One of the bus drivers, Steve, became like a baby-sitter to the kids on Macdonald Street. There weren't many passengers on his route, so Steve often let the neighbourhood kids pile into his bus after school during his stopovers. We took turns wearing his bus-driver's hat and tearing off transfers to hand to imaginary customers who got on when we rang the buzzer for imaginary stops. The bus became our clubhouse, and we climbed the poles and practiced knee-hangs from the overhead handrails. Six-

Bus Driver's Assistants
Photo taken by Steve the bus driver

year-old Elsie knew how to make change from Steve's coin machine, Jonathan was an expert on the emergency brake and Patience could operate the switch that opened and closed the doors. Then Steve would drive us around the loop, down to 49th and up Carnarvon to 41st Avenue. Sometimes we even took our dog, Tommy, on these circuits. Two years later BC Electric terminated the bus service for lack of passengers, and we lost our clubhouse.

Over half a century has gone by since those childhood games on Macdonald Street. And in those years Vancouver, like most of the world, has changed dramatically. Yet Macdonald Street seems unchanged. Half a dozen times a week for most of my life, my travels around the city have taken me down Macdonald Street, and each time my childhood memories fondly flash across my windscreen. Except these days I don't need to worry about Tommy the spaniel darting out of the shadows or some kids suddenly pulling-the-rope across the road in front of me.

John David Ross
*For the first four years of my life, I knew Dad only
from this picture on Mum's bedside table*

Chapter 2

Hello Father

My strongest memory from my early childhood was meeting my father for the very first time.

For the first four years of my life my brother Johnny and I were raised by a household of women. The only man in our house was a faded brown and white photo on my mum's bedside table. Mum told my brother and me that the man in the photograph was our father and that he was far away fighting Germans. The man in the photo was wearing a uniform with shiny buttons and a peaked cap on his head like policemen wore. His mouth wore a broad toothy smile. Settled on his rather large nose was a pair of glasses, and behind them his eyes sparkled. Despite the stiffness of his uniform the man in the portrait looked wise and kind.

I remember the day clearly. It was springtime. There were blossoms on the fruit trees in our back yard. A taxi drove up our driveway and out stepped a tall man wearing a khaki army coat. He had a peaked cap like a policeman. It was the same cap as in the portrait on my mother's bedside table. It was the same man.

This was the man that Mum was always knitting socks for and writing letters to. This was the moment she'd spent so much time

Mum with Johnny and newborn Bobby *(me)* — 1940
The four-year vigil begins

preparing us for. She was so happy to have our father home. But I felt strange. I sensed that my life was about to change and I wasn't sure if it was a good thing.

My brother and I stared in uncomfortable silence as the stranger with the familiar face entered our home. It was a momentous occasion that we had been anticipating with uncertainty and apprehension. The man walked over to my brother and shook his hand, and then he took mine and said "Hello, Bobby."

No hugs! No kisses! No tears of joy! In retrospect, this was a pretty good clue that ours is a family not inclined to display its emotions.

Memories can become distorted over time, but fifty years after this event I had an opportunity to read the war-time diaries written by my dad's sister (my Aunt Kay) who spent the war years in England. Her entry for May 15, 1945 validates my recollection of my first meeting with my father. She wrote:

> *A letter from my father* [my grandfather] *telling me of Jack's* [my father] *reception at home by his two little sons — the younger* [me] *whom he has never seen. They were painting when Jack came into the room. They both got up and went up and shook hands with him politely and then went back to their painting. I am so happy Jack's war is over and that he is home again after five years.*

Who was my father? Where did he come from? Our first Ross ancestor to emigrate to Canada was Dad's great grandfather, who lived in the parish of Edderton in Ross-shire, north of Inverness. In the early 1800s, Scottish lords were evicting the peasants from their lands to make way for larger more profitable tracts to graze their sheep. Facing the choice of a desolate future eking out a life between the mountains and the sea in this foggy patch of Scotland, John Munro Ross chose to join the tide of emigration to the new world. In 1830, as old as the century, he bought passage in a sailing ship bound for America.

After a brief stint as a contractor building railways and canals in Massachusetts, Ross purchased 400 acres of land at Embro, near London, Ontario. He cleared the land and built a grist mill and a farm, which he called *Scotia Farm*. This was to be the home of four generations of Rosses, including my grandfather (also named John Munro), who was born there in 1877.[1]

In 1899 my grandfather volunteered with the first Canadian contingent to join the Boer War. The first of our family to go to war, my 22-year-old grandfather started a military tradition that was to have a significant effect on my life.

In 1909 my dad, John David Ross, was born in Woodstock,

---

[1] The history of the Rosses is told in *The Rosses of Embro*, a chronicle sponsored by my cousin Charles Loewen and privately published in 1989.

Ontario (near Embro). A couple of years later his family moved to Vancouver. At the age of four he was sent to Crofton House School (which is today an exclusive girls school, but in those days apparently took in young boys as well).

At the outbreak of World War I my grandfather Ross went overseas to fight again. He commanded a brigade of the Canadian Corps at the Battle of Vimy Ridge, a horrendous battle in which the success of Canadian troops is said to have been a defining event in Canadian nationhood. When he was wounded in 1918, his family went to England so that they could all be together during his six-month convalescent leave.[2]

While in England, my dad and his sister, Aunt Kay, were sent to English boarding schools.[3] Dad's boarding school burned to the ground one night, and he barely escaped from his dormitory with nothing but his pyjamas. For the rest of his life my father would be paranoid about fire. (I remember as a child the day he bought a heavy rope and secured it to the hot-water heater in our upstairs bedroom, and for the rest of my childhood frequently gave my brother and me instructions in the use of the rope, should a fire trap us in our bedroom.)

When the First World War ended, Dad's family returned to Canada, moving to Victoria in 1920. His parents shipped him off to boarding school at Shawnigan Lake. My poor dad — almost his entire childhood was spent in boarding schools. He went on to graduate from Royal Military College in Kingston Ontario in 1929 with a degree in Engineering, followed by a law degree from Osgoode Hall in Toronto.

During the Depression of the 1930s my dad practiced law in Vancouver. At a New Year's Eve party in West Vancouver he met my mother, and they were married at Ashcroft Ranch, near Cache Creek, BC, in 1936.

---

[2] Grandfather Major General J.M. Ross died in 1959. He is buried at Embro, Ontario.

[3] Dad's sister, my Aunt Kay, married Charles Loewen, whose military career commenced with 17 years as an artillery officer in the British Army on India's North West Frontier. After a distinguished military career, Sir Charles Loewen retired as adjutant general of the British Army in 1959.

The Yard-Maintenance Crew — 1942
As the men of the house, Johnny and I took our duties seriously

Dad joined the militia as a gunner and at the outbreak of World War II in 1939 he was adjutant of the 15th (Vancouver) Coast Brigade Royal Canadian Artillery. He was sent overseas in May 1940 and spent the next four years training in England. On D-Day, the 6th of June 1944, he embarked with the 13th Field Regiment in the invasion fleet to Normandy. As an artillery officer, Capt. Ross' job was to get ashore as quickly as possible in order to direct the artillery fire from the battle ships.

He was one of the first ashore on Juno Beach.

Dad never talked about his war-time experiences, but on one memorable occasion he recounted for me those dreadful moments when his landing craft hit the beach and dropped its ramp. With the ramp no longer providing protection, enemy machine-gun bullets ricocheted around the steel interior of the hull. As the amphibious tank with which the soldiers shared the landing craft trundled away toward the beach, the soldiers were exposed to the murderous fire. I asked him

The Victory Henhouse — 1943
Johnny and me feeding our family's source of war-time eggs:
Veronica, Cocoa, and Priscille

how scared he was, but he would only say that they had no choice but to wade ashore. In a matter of seconds he had the doubtful distinction of being one of the first Canadian officers wounded. He received three wounds, and recalls how every soldier who scurried past him on the beach that morning gave him a pain-killing shot of morphine.

Dad was evacuated to England and didn't rejoin his regiment until the autumn of 1944 at the Leopold Canal, when the Canadian Army was clearing the approaches to the Port of Antwerp. He carried on until just before the crossing of the Rhine. Finally, in the spring of 1945, after five years away from his family, Dad was given leave to return home. By this time I was 4 years old, and he had never seen me.

My dad wasn't used to kids. He'd spent most of his life in boarding schools and army barracks, and had little experience in the dynamics of family households. He didn't tolerate nonsense. Barely a month after we met each other, I infuriated him by gaily calling out "Hi, sloppy Joe giggling girtle." He responded by applying Mum's silver-handled hairbrush to my backside. I'd never seen anyone so angry. I was terrified. I'd never been spanked before. He hit me so hard that the hairbrush broke. And that made him even angrier. So he gave me half a dozen more good whacks with his hand.

I never spoke disrespectfully to him again.[4]

Some time later Johnny confided in me that the soldiers received schooling on the troop ships coming home from the war. The dads were told that their kids wouldn't turn out to be as well-behaved as the letters from the mums suggested. They were told they'd need patience in understanding their children.

Perhaps my dad missed that class.

My poor dad. As a kid I worked hard to meet his high expectations for spit and polish. Nonetheless I got the occasional spanking, and unfortunately spankings stick in my memory as much as the times of laughter with my dad.

I never sat on my father's shoulders, nor walked hand in hand with him down a country lane. We never made a model boat or flew a kite together. We never kicked a ball or played catch. But I cherished our family dinners together every Saturday evening, and have the fondest memories of our family parlour games like charades and fizz-fuzz.

Dad and I developed great respect for one another. My greatest sadness is that I never knew how to tell him I loved him until the last time I saw him alive. He passed away in 1980, and is buried in the family plot at Mountain View Cemetery.

I may not have glimpsed the world from atop my dad's shoulders, but I learned volumes about it from just listening to him. He taught me respect and integrity and the importance of believing in something greater than myself.

---

[4] My niece, Margaret, who was named after my mother, now owns that silver hair brush. It's adorned with a silver sleeve which covers the break in the handle. I hope that nowadays it is only used for brushing hair.

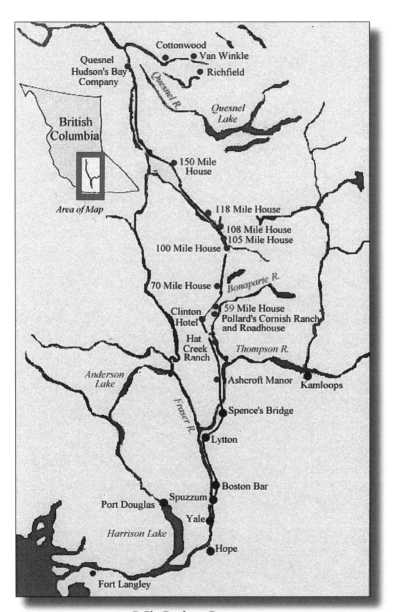

BC's Cariboo Country

After Dad returned from the war, our family spent the next few summer holidays taking car trips through British Columbia

Chapter 3

A Taste for Travel

Most people in the 1940s and early '50s were not interested in (nor able to) travel for pleasure. After the war, the baby boomers were busy starting families and making mortgage payments. Money was scarce, and vacation allowances were short. Tourism wasn't yet part of the culture. For kids, summer holidays were just more time to spend at home in the neighbourhood, climbing trees or playing baseball, or, if you were lucky, a bus ride to the beach for the day.

But I was one of the fortunate, because the first few summers after my dad returned from the war, we spent his annual two week vacations on driving holidays through the interior of British Columbia. One year we stayed on a farm at Heffley Creek near Kamloops. Another year we were at Twin Cedars Resort on a remote arm of Shuswap Lake, and other excursions took us through the Okanagan Valley and north along the old Cariboo Wagon Road to Quesnel.

I have fond indelible memories of those trips in my early child-hood. Perhaps it was driving through the interior with my family that fostered my lifelong interest in travel and geography. I had a large map of British Columbia tacked to my bedroom wall, and on it I'd often trace with my finger our summer driving trips, learning the

Cariboo Wagon Road
*Sections of the old wagon road had changed little since its construction
by the Royal Engineers in the 1860s*

mountain ranges and the rivers and memorizing the names of the
towns.

One such vacation was the summer of 1948, when we drove to the
Cariboo to visit the ranches of Mum's childhood. That was the year of
the great flood on the Fraser River, still remembered as the worst on
record. As our 1939 Chevy chugged through the upper Fraser Valley, we
drove through the damage from the disastrous flood. Large chunks of the
road had been washed away. The fields were desolate and empty of live-
stock, and the dirty stains left by the high water on the houses and barns
made their sides look as though they were wrapped in brown paper.

I recalled the loud-speakers on the trucks driving down Macdonald
Street just two months before, pleading for volunteers to join the crews
filling sand bags in the fight against the river. I remembered the photographs covering the front pages of the newspapers, showing only roofs
of barns and houses and lines of tree-tops sticking above the water.
Thousands of farm animals were drowned. Both railways and the
only highway were submerged, cutting Vancouver off from the rest of
Canada for weeks.

Beyond the town of Hope we chugged along in our overloaded car as the road wriggled and twisted through the gorges and precipices of the rugged Fraser Canyon. The forerunner of today's Trans Canada Highway, it was still unpaved and I can remember places where it was supported across the steep rock bluffs by wooden trestles suspended from the cliffs above the rushing river. This road was first constructed in the 1860s by Colonel Moodie and the Royal Engineers who had come from England to reinforce civil administration and to build a wagon road to the Cariboo gold fields. Dad honked the Chevy's horn in case of approaching cars on the switchback corners, and I wondered how a horse-drawn wagon could have made those turns.

Mum's pioneer family had roots in the interior, and she had passed this way many times before. She brought the geography alive by pointing out a never-ending succession of interesting things, like the rough-hewn drying-racks laden with orange carcasses of salmon dip-netted by the Natives in the river below. Or the tiny old church of St John the Divine in Yale, where Mum said that her Aunt Ida was the first white baby to be christened.

My brother and I were never bored on these long drives through British Columbia. The jolting and swerving on the rough and torturous

Our '39 Chevy
Selecting the campsite

23

road kept us in touch with the land as we eagerly watched for land-marks and points of interest. And there was always the competition for the first to spot a deer or a bear or other wildlife. Those family drives taught me to love the journey as much as the destination.

Years later I was to drive my own kids many times through the Fraser Canyon. I tried to share with them my mother's stories about the old landmarks, but by then the traffic was so fast and the highway so straight and removed from the river that the old landmarks and points of interest no longer seemed relevant. The scenery couldn't hold my children's interest. Today it seems we engage less with the passing countryside, and instead need distractions within the car, like music and movies. But not me, not with my training from those early family drives — even when I travel by airplane, I'm the only guy on the plane at 30,000 feet with his face pressed to the window, looking for land-marks and points of interest.

Mum's mother and aunts had lived in Yale and in Spuzzum when they were little girls in the 1880s during the time that their father, Henry Cambie, was in charge of construction of the Canadian Pacific Railway through the Fraser Canyon. Today only a dozen people live in Spuzzum, and perhaps a hundred in Yale, but during the Cariboo gold rush and the boom days of the railway construction, Spuzzum was much bigger; while Yale at that time was said to have been home to several thousand pioneers.

At Spuzzum we stopped on the old suspension bridge and peered down through the open grating of the deck at the churning river below. At Hell's Gate we hiked down to the brand-new concrete fish ladders which were expected to bring the return of the once-mighty salmon runs. Mum told us about a big steam-driven paddle-wheeler that was built in Spuzzum when her mother lived there, which had actually worked its way upstream through the boiling rapids of Hell's Gate.

At the town of Lytton, Mum and Dad disappeared into the hotel beer parlour for a cool draught. In those days liquor wasn't served in restaurants, nor could it be obtained on Sundays. Prohibition hadn't ended very long before, and if my parents wanted to enjoy a cool drink,

Fishing in Hat Creek
Johnny and me with our catch of brook trout

beer parlours were their only option. Natives weren't allowed in beer parlours and men weren't allowed to drink with unescorted women. Johnny and I waited outside in the car, trying to imagine what sins were being committed behind the segregated doors marked "Men" and "Ladies and Escorts!"

In the last mile or two before the Ashcroft turnoff, the highway passes through the old Cornwall Ranch, which was homesteaded in 1862 by my Uncle Fitz's father. It was here that Aunt Mabel and Uncle Fitz had raised nine children, and here at the Cornwall Ranch that Mum had spent her childhood summers. She and Dad had been married at the old ranch house in 1936. Mum spoke with nostalgia of those days in her youth when she rode across the surrounding hills with the Cornwall boys and saddled up each autumn to help with the cattle round-ups.

Further up the road, near 150 Mile House, one of Fitz Cornwall's sons, my cousin Hugh, owned and operated the Onward Ranch. We stayed overnight on the ranch. Before supper, I helped the Chinese cook kill a chicken for the pot. He strung it up by its legs and pierced its brain with his knife. With blood gushing from its squawking beak it flapped its wings for an eternity, while my stomach churned at the sight and the sound of its death. I helped pluck it — but I didn't eat supper that night. And if I'd known that a diet without meat would some day be fashionable, I would have become a vegetarian then and there.

That year's Cariboo adventure included my first and only camping experience with my parents. Camping was something that did not come naturally to Dad. I think his only experience in the outdoors had been in army bivouacs. Before we set up the tent, he made us take a shovel and mattock and dig a latrine so deep that the poop from an entire army wouldn't have filled it in a month. Then we constructed a fire pit — and cleared a ten-foot swath down to bare earth to contain any sparks. We lugged water from the creek in canvas army buckets for fire suppression and set up a canvas basin for washing. We pitched the canvas tent on a ridge pole cut from a tree.

It was exhausting. I thought Dad was going to make us build a stockade and clear sight lines for the guns! But he sensed our lack of enthusiasm, and served us a plate of Spam instead. A left-over war ration, Spam didn't even need to be cooked. Mum's response to the Spam was to bait a hook with grass-hoppers and worms and teach us to catch fish on a line dangled from a willow pole. We caught several little brown brook trout and learned to clean out their guts before frying them over Dad's fire. Great, another meal that had been alive and wriggling only an hour before. I added fresh fish to my most-hated list.

Another thing I learned to hate was mosquitoes. Our tent had no netting and we had no insect repellent. Never since have I encountered such voracious mosquitoes. Dad tried to distract us by saying the little critters were after our noble Scottish blood, which only served to bring out the Irish in Mum.

As we digested our evening meal around the campfire, Mum told

Roadside Picnic Lunch
Dad, Johnny and me in a field near Ashcroft

us about the pioneer days at the Cornwall ranch, when coyotes were hunted with hounds[5] that had been brought in sailing ships all the way around Cape Horn from England in the 1860s. Later, as we were serenaded to sleep by the yipping of coyotes in the surrounding hills, my mind played with her description of the hunt, complete with the scarlet-coated Indian boy dressed as the hunt master, mounted on horseback and blowing the bugle!

When we broke camp a couple of days later, Dad made us fill in the privy and bury all our garbage and then pour half of Hat Creek over the cold remnants of the campfire. No enemy would ever to be able to trace us.

Our parents never took us camping again. But the experience was unforgettable.

---

[5] My mother subsequently compiled the story of the coyote hunts from Clement Cornwall's diaries.

Robert Garnett Tatlow
My mother's father — entrepreneur and politician
(1908 portrait by Spy in *Vanity Fair)*

Chapter 4

The Pioneers

Today, almost half the people in Vancouver speak English as a second language. Almost everyone you run into has moved here from somewhere else. Meeting an adult who was born in Vancouver is so unusual that the moment is almost cause for celebration. "You were actually born here?" "No kidding!" "Wow, that's rare!"

I am one of that rare species. Even more unusual, my mother and her mother before her were also born in Vancouver. Mum's father and her mother's father both moved west to settle in the almost-empty province of British Columbia in the 1870s. In my childhood I spent time with elderly relatives who talked incessantly about the "early days." And, unlike my own children, I loved it when one of my elders would say, "Bobby, did I ever tell you what it was like in the old days . . ." And off we'd go on some magical trip down memory lane.

I realize now that it was those tales of the early days of British Columbia, told with the intimacy of first-hand knowledge, that stirred my imagination and awakened my lifelong love for history. The countless anecdotes told by my great aunts and great uncles about little details in the lives of their pioneer friends gave me a sense of my roots and the feeling that my family was part of the history of British Columbia.

My first ancestor on my mother's side of the family to arrive in the New World was Henry Cambie, my mother's grandfather. He came from Ireland.

My mother had in her possession an old blueprint of our Cambie family tree. As I was growing up I often traced the branches with my finger all the way back to David Cambie, who was a colonel in Queen Elizabeth's army and had charge of one of the ships that sailed against the Spanish Armada in 1588. Another Cambie was an officer in Cromwell's army during the campaign in Ireland in 1640 and was given land, from which the poor Irish peasants were evicted.

My great-grandfather Henry Cambie was born in County Tipperary in 1836. During his youth, the potato famine of 1845 to 1849 decimated the Irish populace and caused a flood of emigration, but the aristocratic Cambies on their vast estate at Coolbahn didn't suffer the terrible plight of the Catholic countryside. Many of Henry Cambie's descendants have returned to visit the old Cambie home, which still stands on a hillside overlooking Lough Derg. My wife Sandra and I went there in 1992 and had tea with Mrs Sterling, whose family is the second to own the estate since the Cambies left. For me it was exciting to connect with my great grandfather's boyhood memories which I had read in his journals. But the family's fortified estate left in me a sadness about the centuries of cruel oppression that my invading ancestors inflicted on the Catholic Irish peasants.

By an extraordinary coincidence, our visit in 1992 uncovered Sandra's previously undiscovered family roots. Not thirty kilometres away, in a desolate windswept field beyond the sight of any road, stood a burned hulk called *Otway Castle*. Until this trip, Sandra had no idea where in Ireland her ancestors lived. Records in the local archives confirmed not only her heritage, but also that in the 1800s one of her Otway forebears had married one of us Cambies in a nearby church.

Great-grandfather Henry Cambie emigrated with his parents to Canada in 1852. He obtained employment as an engineer on the Grand Trunk Railway and later as a railway surveyor and engineer in Ontario and Nova Scotia. In 1874 he was sent to British Columbia to explore and survey various proposed routes for the railway which had been promised to British Columbia when it joined Confederation three years before. At the time of his arrival on the west coast there was as yet no settlement where Vancouver is now, other than a scattering of Indian villages and a cluster of shacks called Hastings Mill surrounding an isolated wharf on Burrard Inlet.

Over the next few years Cambie surveyed, by canoe and by horse, three routes to the ocean and three potential terminals for the railroad. Farthest north, he explored the route favoured by Sir Stanford Fleming, who proposed that the rail terminus be located at the mouth of the Skeena River (the future site of Prince Rupert), because that route involved an easier passage through the Rocky Mountains and a shorter crossing of the Pacific to destinations in the Orient.

Another possible terminus was Bute Inlet; and Cambie's diaries[6] tell a harrowing tale of his exploration of that route, down the Homathco River to tidewater in 1876. He was the first unescorted white visitor to enter this valley from the Chilcotin after the massacre of the surveyor Waddington and his entire party of sixteen men, ten years before. The Natives did their best to intimidate Cambie and his French-Canadian packer by galloping alongside on their horses and stopping suddenly, throwing their horses on their haunches and making threatening gestures. Cambie's own words describe the moment:

> *No one spoke — we kept on our way, a fast walk, and soon left*
> *them behind. I confess that, knowing these men to be of the same*
> *families who had murdered Waddington's party ten years before,*
> *it gave a cold chill down my spine, but I kept outwardly calm,*
> *knowing that any sign of weakness would be very bad.*

Cambie recommended Burrard Inlet for the railway's terminus, despite concerns that proximity to the American border would make the

---

[6] The original field books of these surveys, written in Cambie's distinct flowing handwriting, were stacked in our basement for many years. They make fascinating reading. I donated them to the Vancouver Archives in 1995.

The Last Spike — "The Great Canadian Photograph"
Great-grandfather Henry Cambie (white circle) watches the completion of his work

railway vulnerable if Canada should again go to war with the United States. As we know, Burrard Inlet was finally chosen, and more tonnage is now shipped through Vancouver than any other port on the west coast.

In 1880, Cambie took charge of building the Canadian Pacific Railway through the Fraser Canyon. His field books, diaries and notes record in gripping detail all the activities associated with the enormous difficulties of constructing a railway through the rugged confines of those precipitous gorges. And all without the assistance of modern excavation and tunnelling equipment. Descriptions of surveying, designing, blasting, tunnelling, trestle-building, and laying steel are salted with insights into the living and working conditions of the labourers, whom the contractor Onderdonk imported from San Francisco and China. The diaries also provide fascinating glimpses into family life on the frontier.

When the rails from the east met the line from the west at Craigellachie, in the mountains near Shuswap Lake on November 7,

1885, Henry Cambie was present. In the well-known photograph of the driving of the last spike — "The Great Canadian Photograph," as Pierre Berton calls it — great-grandfather Henry Cambie is the guy with the white beard, black moustache and bowler hat standing directly behind the small boy.

He continued in the employ of the Canadian Pacific Railway until his retirement in 1919, at the age of 83. Henry Cambie is buried in the family plot at Mountain View Cemetery in Vancouver. Cambie Street in Vancouver is named after him.[7]

Henry Cambie raised five children, the eldest of whom was my grandmother Elizabeth. During the construction of the railway in the Fraser Canyon, the Cambie family lived in Yale and Spuzzum. Today, both these places are ghost towns by comparison, but during the 1880s their populations were in the thousands. The Cambies moved to Vancouver and built a house in 1887 at the northeast corner of Georgia and Thurlow, where the MacMillan Bloedel office tower stands today. In 1894 Elizabeth married Robert Garnett Tatlow, who had emigrated from Ireland in 1871.

* * *

Robert Garnett Tatlow, my mother's father, was born at Scava in County Cavin in Northern Ireland in 1854. At the age of seventeen he declined an opportunity to be apprenticed to a lawyer, and sailed off to Montreal, where he worked in the office of a steamship company.

He joined the militia and in 1879 was posted to the far side of Canada, to an artillery regiment newly assigned to Victoria. At that time the non-native population of Victoria was only about six thousand pioneers.

Unable to support a wife on the meagre pay of an artillery captain,

---

[7] The story of Henry Cambie's life was featured in a series of articles written by Noel Robinson and published in *MacLean's* Magazine in December 1923, January and February 1924. Cambie Street in Vancouver is named after him. He had five children—the oldest, Elizabeth, was my mum's mother.

he accepted a position as aide-de-camp to the lieutenant-governor of British Columbia. His new salary enabled him to get married, and his first daughter, my Aunt Mabel, was born in their Pandora Street cottage in 1882. Grandfather Tatlow remained secretary to Lieutenant-Governor Cornwall until 1886, the year after the Canadian Pacific Railway was completed across Canada to Port Moody.

With the arrival of the new railway, Vancouver became a boomtown, so Tatlow moved there and entered the real estate business, at which he was very successful.

His wife, Aunt Mabel's mother, died from injuries sustained in a fall in 1886. A board crossing a creek broke under her weight during a picnic on the north shore of Burrard Inlet. Eight years later, grandfather Tatlow married his second wife, Elizabeth Cambie, who would become my grandmother.

Robert Tatlow was a founder of the BC Telephone Company. He was the MLA for Vancouver and in 1902 he became the Minister of Finance and Agriculture in the cabinet of Sir Richard McBride. His cabinet responsibilities required that he move his family back to Victoria, where they bought a house on Rockland Avenue.

He had four children with Elizabeth Cambie, the youngest being my mother, who was born in 1909. Unfortunately, my mother never got to know her father, as Robert Tatlow was killed when his horse bolted, throwing him from his carriage two months before Mum was born in June 1909.

There were several tragedies in my mother's family. A few years after her father's death, which had been a terrible blow to her pregnant mother, Mum's older brother, Jack, was killed in the Great War. Jack had been a scholar, a gifted athlete and, before his death in 1918, the youngest major in the British Army. These premature deaths sent my grandmother Elizabeth into depression, from which I gather she never recovered. Then, in 1935, Mum's older sister Helen, who was an excellent tennis player and horsewoman, was thrown from her horse and killed on Christmas Day. My grandmother's depression worsened and she died in 1943, before I had a chance to know her.

Margaret Garnett Tatlow
Mum at age 19

Mum lived on Cartier Avenue in Vancouver, and attended the old Prince of Wales High School (as well as a year at Vernon Prep School in Vernon). I think she had a privileged childhood, complete with a Chinese houseboy. She often shared with me her fond memories of school vacations in the Cariboo, riding horses across the range at the Cornwall's ranch near Ashcroft, and summers camping at *Finnerty*, a family-owned seashore property in Saanich.

It was at the Ashcroft ranch that she and Dad were married in 1936. In the 1930s my grandmother bought the house on Macdonald Street where I was to grow up but, not long after my brother and I were born, our grandmother was moved to a nursing home.

With my father away at the war, and my mother's time absorbed by her own mother's illness and the demands of a large house and garden, Johnny and I were looked after by a nanny. Our nanny was a Japanese Canadian who, for some reason, was given the unlikely name, "Hodges." But after the Japanese attacked Pearl Harbour, Hodges was sent away to an internment camp and we never saw her again.

My mother loved the outdoors. She knew everything about animals and birds and trees and flowers. Our home on Macdonald Street had almost an acre of property, and during the war years Mum (with the help of our Chinese gardener, Ho Loo) grew most of our fresh fruit and vegetables. Eggs were scarce during the war, so Mum

35

acquired chickens and we produced our own. When Johnny and I were small we sometimes stayed with relatives who owned farms, and Mum frequently took us on excursions to the beach or the mountains or the woods, where she shared with us her love of nature.

Another strong memory I have of my mother when I was small was our bed-time stories together. Mostly she read to us about animals, like *Black Beauty*, *The Call of the Wild*, and Earnest Thompson Seton's *Lives of the Hunted*. Mum had a way of bringing the animals to life — she gave them dignity, made them gentle creatures with noble virtues. From Mum I learned at an early age to love animals.

I'll never forget one example of how her early parenting prepared me for life. I was to write a test as a five-year-old to determine whether I should be allowed to enter the first year of elementary school with six-year-old kids. I was one of two dozen aspiring young geniuses whose birthdays fell between the beginning of the school year and the end of December. A teacher handed us each a sheaf of papers and instructed us to draw lines above, around and through pictures of various objects like horses and chickens and vegetables. I found the test ridiculously easy — thanks to the countless hours that Mum had spent introducing my brother and me to the wonders of the world. But in the seats around me, I noticed that other kids were having trouble figuring which end of the pencil to use or which page we were on, or whether a chicken was a duck.

After my dad returned from the war, I don't recall spending much time with my mother. Our family ate breakfast separately, and said goodbye as we disappeared separately out the front door each morning; Dad walked up to 41st Avenue to catch the Macdonald bus to his law practice downtown, and Johnny and I walked or cycled to school. Household chores and grocery shopping took up most of Mum's days.

The only time we had together as a family was suppertime. Until I was 13 or 14 years old, the evening meal with my family was a significant event. Hands washed, hair combed, good posture and, most important, proper table manners. Mum's home-cooked meals were never elegant but always tasty — meat, potato and one vegetable — and a homemade dessert. But most important was the family conversation. Everyone at the table felt respected and valued.

Like most other families, we never went out for dinner; and in those days there was no such thing as take-out or food delivery. On Saturday nights we always had a roast of beef or lamb with roast potatoes and green beans or fresh peas (in season). Oh how I looked forward to Saturday dinners — Dad carving the roast and telling jokes at the head of our antique dining room table, Mum serving the vegetables and ladling gravy or mint sauce onto our steaming plates, and Johnny across the table trying his best to eat with his mouth closed. And after dinner we'd play parlour games in the living room, like fizz-fuzz, consequences, or dominoes. If we were really lucky, and Dad was into his cups, he'd sing one or two of his old barrack-room army songs — to the delight of our spaniel, Tommy, who'd throw back his head and howl.

Mum, like Dad, never hugged me. I don't even remember being kissed by my mother. Perhaps it was their Victorian up-bringing, perhaps displaying affection was not normal for the times. I don't think my brother and I were over-indulged, but I always knew that Mum loved and cared deeply for us. She was quick to show us that there was a right way and a wrong way to do things, like holding a knife and fork, or speaking proper grammar. She figured if you took care of the little things, the big things in life would look after themselves. And Mum always made me feel secure, supported and empowered.

Several landmarks in Vancouver, including Tatlow Park, are named after Mum's father who, like Mum, is buried in the family plot at Mountain View Cemetery in Vancouver.

Over the years I often visit the Tatlow and Cambie gravesites. The Celtic cross above the Cambies and the pink granite obelisk over the Tatlows occupy a prominent position, side by side, looking out over the city my forefathers helped carve out of the wilderness. They always instill in me a sense of pride for the contribution that my family made to the history of my province.

The Cucumber Tree
Fifty-year reunion

Chapter 5

The Cucumber Tree

Nowadays you don't see kids in trees. Watch a kid start to climb a tree and you'll likely hear a parent shouting "Be careful!" "You might fall!" "You'll hurt yourself!" When we were kids we spent half our time more than ten feet above the ground. Sometimes we did fall, sometimes we did hurt ourselves. But how boring would a childhood be without trees to climb.

On Macdonald Street the lots were big and trees were everywhere. Every yard had a favourite climbing tree, and on the undeveloped properties there were forests of giant evergreens, firs and cedars, some a hundred-feet tall. Behind the Silbernagel's house there was even an orchard which covered a third of an acre and was home to two dozen mature fruit trees — apples, pears, plums and cherries. Many a lazy summer afternoon was whiled away in the branches in Mrs Turvey's orchard, gorging ourselves on cherries and unripe plums. And Mrs Turvey, like most of the owners in our neighbourhood, didn't object when we kids took over her trees!

Our first tree was a weeping willow with a massive trunk and solid limbs that towered above our garage. Its trunk was impossible to climb. Its lowest branches were over ten feet from the ground. But finally, when I was six or seven, we managed to crack the puzzle by climbing from a wall to the top of the neighbour's fence and then onto the chicken coop, which led to the garage roof. Eventually we bridged the six-foot gap from the roof to the fork of the willow tree with a plank from the hen house. After that, there was no stopping us. The neighbourhood gang spent so much time up there that Mum commenced lunch service, sending up sandwiches on a string in exchange for a promise that we'd come down in time for supper

Sometimes the willow tree was a circus tent and we'd entertain each other with climbing and high-wire acts. Sometimes it was a castle and we'd find ourselves under siege, having to fight off unseen legions of soldiers. Sometimes it was a pirate ship, and the massive limbs pointing skyward were square-rigged masts. When Spanish galleons were sighted we'd rush aloft, some up the mizzen or foremast, others to the crows nest atop the main, armed to the teeth and ready to swing from the rigging, while below on the quarterdeck our crewmates prepared to repel boarders with their cutlasses.

One day we saw a movie about Columbus' voyage to the new world, and the willow tree immediately became the *Santa Maria*. That particular voyage of adventure ended abruptly when Johnny climbed to the maintop and recited the schoolboy refrain "In fourteen hundred and ninety-two, Columbus sailed the ocean blue. He climbed the mast and skinned his ass, and peed all over the crew." Which is precisely what Johnny proceeded to do. And for that he was keel-hauled.

The willow was only one of many trees that helped to shape my childhood. Another was the copper beech in our front yard. I'll never forget how scared we were when six-year old Jonathan lost his grip and fell from its branches to the driveway 10 feet below. I'd never seen a dead person before. We carried him to my mother's bed where, to our surprise, he regained consciousness. Dr MacMillan was summoned — the diagnosis was nothing more serious than a concussion.

The grove of hazelnut trees in our back yard became our special theatre for acrobatics. A cluster of hazelnut trunks grew skyward for fifteen feet before bending over and draping their upper branches onto the lawn. Under this leafy roof a couple of limbs grew horizontally, straight and clear like the high-bar in a gym. We turned knee-hangs, branch-swinging and pole climbs into creative routines and invited the neighbours to the show. We dropped invitations in all the Macdonald Street mail boxes and printed tickets and charged 10 cents admission.

The canopy of leaves high above created an atmosphere like the big top at the circus, and beneath it we set up two rows of lawn chairs for the big performance. Between the death-defying tree-gymnastics of the older kids, chocolate bars and lemonade were sold by six-year-old Elsie and eight-year-old Patience. We were such a hit that we repeated the performance three years in a row. The crowds were so big in the third year (1951) that we put on four performances spread over two days. According to Johnny's diary those four performances brought in a total of $6.73, which we donated to the Children's Hospital.

Ten years later, Jonathan would become a star performer on the high bar with the University of British Columbia's gymnastics team.

The best tree of all, the one which we climbed the most, was the cucumber tree in the Silbernagel's back yard. The cucumber tree was actually a type of magnolia that derives its name from its gherkin-like green seed-pods. It was immense, with enough space in its branches for an entire army of kids to hang out. It reached skyward in three trunks, each supporting its own network of branches, all polished clean by years of climbing. The choice of handgrips and footholds was endless and we climbed like spiders on a giant cobweb in the sky. It was possible for a game of tree-tag to last for hours, high in the branches of this special tree.

From the age of nine until I was fourteen I treasured my hours in that tree, overlooking my childhood domain, free from chores and homework and worldly problems. The cucumber tree became our favourite meeting place. It was here that our little neighbourhood gang met to plan garden raids and war parties and hunting excursions to far-off frog ponds. It was high in the branches of the cucumber tree, each of us perched on our personal branch or wedged securely in our favourite fork, that we shared our hopes and aspirations. We told stories of our summer vacations and complained about homework and teachers and older brothers. Up in our leafy hangout, screened from the outside world, we pondered the world's problems and mulled over mysteries like bees making honey, and baby robins hatching from tiny blue eggs.

And the mystery of sex. According to Johnny's diary, I was twelve years old when John Erskine climbed up our tree and told us an entirely different version of the birds and the bees.

John was a few years older and ran with a fast crowd. He didn't live on our street but sometimes joined us when the fruit was ripe in Mrs Turvey's orchard. Perched on my own special branch, my eyes wide with wonder, I just about lost my grip as John explained girls to us.

Passing through the neighbourhood some fifty years later I noticed that the cucumber tree looked old and stressed. The branches on one side were dead, the leaves tiny and shrivelled. It didn't look like it had long to live. I quickly arranged a get-together of the old gang for a 50th reunion up in its branches. The story of the reunion, and the role that the tree played in our childhood, was beautifully told by *Vancouver Sun* newspaper columnist Pete McMartin in his column published on June 23, 2001. Mr McMartin wrote the story after meeting me beneath the cucumber tree and, with his kind permission, I have reproduced parts of it:

The "Old Gang" Celebrates 50 Years at their Tree of Life in Kerrisdale

by Pete McMartin, *Vancouver Sun*

Every child has a tree in his or her life, and Bob Ross' is a huge, venerable cucumber tree at the corner of Macdonald and 47th in Kerrisdale.

A cucumber tree is a member of the magnolia family, and this one is almost five storeys high with a canopy as big as a cloud. The trunk is so fat it takes four people linking hands to encompass it.

*It is an old tree, with limbs as thick as hydro poles,
and they grow in such a way — horizontally along the
ground and then upward — that they resemble the
cradling of a cupped hand. It is a tree with presence,
and its girth, age and rarity is such that the B.C.
Heritage Trust included it in Vancouver's Heritage
Tree Inventory back in 1982. More important, it's
an excellent climbing tree.*

*Bob, a retired city employee, is now 60, but 50
years ago he used to climb the cucumber tree himself.
It commanded the backyard of the Silbernagels, his
buddies across the street, and he and the Silbernagels
and the rest of the kids that made up the neighbourhood
gang spent hours in the tree, monkeying around.*

*It was their domain — their jungle gym, their fort,
their spy tower, their meeting hall where they convened
to plan their next raid — and it was the high ground
from which they surveyed their childhood kingdom.*

*"You know, you'd sit up there and solve the world's
problems," Bob said.*

*. . . Back then in the gang there was Elsie Wollaston
and Paul Williams, and Paul's brother, Don, and the
Silbernagel brood — Patience, Jon and Stephen.*

*But childhood doesn't last forever, and children must
come down out of the trees to follow more earthbound
pursuits, and the gang grew apart. They all stayed in
Vancouver, except Paul who became a professor of plant
pathology at the University of Wisconsin, Madison, but they
all went on to different careers. As much as 15 years would
go by, Ross said, before he would bump into any of them.*

*He would think about this occasionally when he
mused about his childhood, but it recently came back to
him with a new urgency . . .*

. . . Ross saw his own mortality in that aging tree,

and felt his happy past quickly moving out of memory's reach. He decided he had to do something to celebrate it before it was gone forever.

. . . So, on May 26, at 5 pm, Bob and Paul and Don and Elsie and Patience and Stephen and Jon met in the Silbernagels' old back yard, and with the permission of the present owners, they all clambered up into the branches of the cucumber tree for their 50th anniversary reunion.

. . ."I was impressed," Bob said, "how at home everybody was. Everybody just kind of found their own perch and sat there, and we all talked about our memories."

They recalled "the old hag's woods," the terrifying lair of the local crone. They saw below them the corner of the Silbernagels' house where they played kick-the-can, and saw, too, the old wisteria arbour — still there after 50 years! — in the Wollaston's backyard. They talked about the time they played war with garbage-can lids as shields and garden stakes as swords, and how Don threw a sword at Bob's brother just when he lowered his shield and . . .

. . . . Bob opened a bottle of champagne in the tree and they passed out glasses. They drank a toast to absent loved ones. They drank a toast to good memories. They drank a toast to the tree.

Later, Bob would say: "It'll be like losing an old friend when that tree comes down. When you were up in the canopy, you were shielded from the world."

Indeed, the following year the cucumber tree succumbed to its age. It was deteriorating so rapidly that the owners of the Silbernagels' property had to put it out of its misery. I wasn't there that day, but when I noticed the hole in the sky where it had been I stopped my car and took a look into the yard. The majestic old tree, the core of my childhood, lay in pieces on the ground. The foliage and smaller branches had been taken away and all that remained were 10-foot long sections of the massive trunk, which were stretched out side by side like the bones of some long-dead dinosaur. It made me very sad.

The Macdonald Street Gang
Fifty-year reunion (Brother Johnny absent)

Uncle Fitz and Aunt Mabel
They were a huge inflence on Johnny and me

Chapter 6

Grandma and Grandpa
— Sort Of

My brother Johnny and I never had a chance to know our real grandparents. So that role was taken on by our Aunt Mabel and Uncle Fitz.

Aunt Mabel, Robert Tatlow's first daughter and my mother's half sister, was 28 years older than Mum. She and Uncle Fitz were a huge influence in my early life. They were in their golden years during my early childhood, and took on the role of spoiling my brother and me as though we were their own grand children.

They lived on a small farm that bordered the ocean in south Saanich. Their property was named *Finnerty*, and Johnny and I spent many holidays there during our early years. It was an idyllic location, surrounded by other farms and holly orchards, close to what is now the campus of the University of Victoria.

Many hours I spent in Aunt Mabel's kitchen at *Finnerty*, listening to her raspy voice as she puttered away at her huge wood stove, baking bread and pies; and putting up preserves — peas, beets, pickles, and fruit that we picked from her bountiful garden. I loved the smells of her kitchen — the fresh baking, the wood stove, fresh cut flowers in a vase on the table. And I can still hear the jingling of the old country phone on the wall, with its different combinations of long and short rings for the other parties that shared her line. I love my memories of her plump little figure in an ageless polka-dot dress, her silver hair knotted in a tight bun and her tiny rimless spectacles perched on the tip of her nose, as she puttered around the cold draughty house, dispensing little homilies and tales of her pioneer friends.

Aunt Mabel told us many stories of the "old days" in British Columbia. She was four years old when the Great Fire raged across most of Vancouver in 1886, killing 16 people. The lumber which her father had purchased for building his house on Alexander Street was destroyed in the Great Fire.

She remembered other fires as well. One night she was carried from her bed, a thick veil wrapped around her head to protect her eyes from the cinders. The family's valuables were tied in shawls and lowered into deep holes beneath the wood-plank sidewalk. While most of the men fought the fires, one or two stayed back to row the women and children out into Burrard Inlet if the fire came dangerously close.

She also told us about the arrival of Engine #374 pulling the first regular passenger train across Canada in May of 1887.

As a young lady she enjoyed the social scene in the capital city of Victoria. She studied in Germany, and traveled extensively throughout Europe, before marrying Uncle Fitz and settling down to run a cattle ranch in the Cariboo.

Uncle Fitz was also fun to be with, and how the time flew when my brother and I explored the barns and sheds with him, or hung by our knees from the branches of fruit trees, or rode *Driftwood,* the life-sized rocking horse. I helped him with the farm chores, searching the barn for eggs from the little bantam chickens, weeding the vegetable garden and walking hand-in-hand to the neighbour's farm for fresh milk or out to the road to check the mailbox each day. He made me feel that I was indispensable to the running of the farm.

Uncle Fitz introduced Johnny and me to the seashore. We spent hours at the tidal pools amongst the barnacle-covered rocks below the cottage, scooping up bull-heads and crabs as they scurried for shelter in

Me, Johnny and "Driftwood"
A wonderful memory of "Finnerty"

the seaweed. We saw how hermit crabs set up house in abandoned sea-shells, and how the delicate sea anemones retract their tentacles when prodded. The water was too cold for swimming, but we learned about the ebb and flow of the tides, as we hunted for agates and driftwood treasures at the pebble beach. Uncle Fitz taught us to listen for the deep engine-throb of passing tugs and freighters, and the quieter CPR passenger boats — the *Princess Charlotte* and *Princess Louise*, and to stay clear of the pounding waves on the beach a few minutes after they'd passed. I'll always remember the tinkling of the pebbles as each wave receded. I can still smell the tang of the salt ocean and the seaweed uncovered by the dropping tides.

I can also smell Uncle Fitz's pipe. He often reclined in his big easy chair in the sunroom, wearing a tired old tweed jacket, smoke from his pipe curling up through his Joseph Stalin moustache, while the console radio vibrated to the dance tunes of Tommy Dorsey. It was in the sunroom that he taught us to play crib and chess. He made me feel that whatever I said was important. He helped me make the big decisions — like what to be when I grew up. One year we decided I would join the circus and become an acrobat. On another visit we decided I should be an astronomer (but I remember not being entirely sure just what an astronomer does).

Uncle Fitz's stories about his heritage were as fascinating as Aunt Mabel's. He was the third son of another pioneer family. His father, Clement Francis Cornwall, emigrated to Canada in 1862, via Panama and San Francisco. Clement Cornwall and his brother joined the throngs of young adventurers seeking their fortunes on the gold fields of the Fraser River and the Cariboo.

In San Francisco, Clement bought a horse for $60 and paid another $15 for its passage to Victoria. He bought a second horse in Victoria for $130, loaded it with provisions from the Hudson's Bay Company store and set out with his brother Henry for the interior of British Columbia. At that time there was no road through the Fraser River canyon, so their journey took them from New Westminster via the Harrison/Douglas Trail up Harrison Lake and Lilloett Lake to the town of Lilloett, situated beyond the impassable canyons of the Fraser River.

It's not clear why they didn't continue on to the goldfields, but at some point they decided to take up farming instead. They found some promising land on a bench west of the Thompson River, above what would later become the city of Ashcroft, and pre-empted (initially) 320 acres.

In short order the Cornwalls built a cabin and began raising live-stock. Eventually they built a large ranch house and operated a sawmill, a gristmill and a road house (which is still open today as *Ashcroft Manor*, on the Trans Canada Highway south of Cache Creek.) Instead of digging for gold, the Cornwall brothers made money catering to the needs of the thousands of hungry miners already at the Cariboo diggings, and the hordes of eager prospectors swarming north along the newly constructed Cariboo Wagon Road, one portion of which was built right through their ranch.[8]

In 1864 Clement Cornwall was elected to the legislative council

---

[8] The early days of the Cornwall Ranch are described in CF Cornwall's diary, of which several family members have copies.

of the Colony of British Columbia, and later he became a senator, representing the new province of British Columbia in the federal government. In 1881 Cornwall was appointed Lieutenant-Governor of BC. Uncle Fitz was born in 1880, in Ashcroft.

Aunt Mabel and Uncle Fitz may have first met when her father Robert Tatlow (my grandfather) was aide-de-camp to Lieutenant Governor Cornwall in the 1880s. I know from stories which she later recounted about the parties and fancy balls at Government House after the turn of the century that Aunt Mabel was quite prominent in social circles in Victoria before being invited to visit the Cornwalls' ranch at Ashcroft in 1907. She fell in love with Fitz and they were married the following year.

Aunt Mabel raised nine children at the ranch. One of her daughters, Evelyn, was the same age as my mother and they became best friends. Mom spent all her childhood summers and most fall round-ups and Christmas holidays at the Cornwall Ranch. During the Depression of the 1930s, the ranch fell on hard times, and Aunt Mabel and Uncle Fitz sold it and moved to the cottage in Saanich — *Finnerty* — which my grandfather, Robert Tatlow, had built as a summer home many years earlier.

Uncle Fitz died in 1960. Aunt Mabel lived on as sharp as a tack until she passed away in 1974 at the age of ninety-two. They are buried on a wind-swept hillside in the Cariboo, in a lovely little family cemetery near the site of the old homestead on the Cornwall Ranch near Ashcroft. When each of their children subsequently passed away, my wife Sandra and I attended their graveside ceremonies at that historic site. And each time I remembered with great fondness their influence on my life.

The *Finnerty* property was eventually subdivided. Single family homes and Locarno Lane cover the old farm, while the seafront was sold to the University of Victoria, which uses it for research in marine biology.

Cornwall Avenue in Vancouver is named after Clement Cornwall.

Our Cliff-Top Fort at Pasley — 1952
*Perched atop a cliff with a commanding view,
and entered by dropping from a tree through a trapdoor in its roof,
this fort was impregnable to our island enemies*

Chapter 7

Urban Warriors

It seems to me that between the ages of 8 and 12 we were always building a fort somewhere, or defending a fort, or preparing to raid someone else's fort.

In most neighbourhoods, small groups of pre-teens had hide-outs. They were tucked away in overgrown vacant lots or ravines and woodlands, never visible from streets or houses. They were concealed in bushes or up in trees or behind garden sheds. They were built of old boards or branches or when it was winter, chunks of snow.

Half our waking moments seemed to be consumed in plotting how to destroy the other guys' fortresses or developing more secure defences for our own strongholds. We probably didn't spend as much time skirmishing with each other as I remember, but those pitched battles against the Elm Street Gang or the upper classmen at Kerrisdale Elementary sure got my juices running.

I think it started with snow forts. In the late 1940s Vancouver had some heavy snowfalls. For four or five winters in a row, the snow was deep and lay around for several weeks. When we tired of making snowmen we progressed to igloos and snow forts. Sometimes we built a simple wall of snow perhaps three feet high, and defended it against snowball attacks by opposing forces.

Whenever a group of boys congregated around snow forts, it was a recipe for a snowball fight. Nowadays schools try to ban throwing snowballs on their premises but, in my childhood, school recesses on snowy days featured some pretty intense battles. When the bell rang we'd rush outside and charge to the battlefield, packing snowballs on the run.

The neat thing about snowball fights is that you either win or you lose. There are no arguments like the "I got yuh! . . . No yuh dinnint" of "cowboys and indians."[9] There is no compromise — a snowball splat in your face speaks for itself.

I remember being badly beaten in one particular snowball fight when I was in Grade 3. We were trading volleys with some bigger Grade 4 kids when suddenly they charged and bashed down our fortification. I fled in terror but was caught from behind and flung to the ground where some goon twice my size gave me the mother of all face washes. I struggled to my feet and stood there sobbing, wiping away the ice and snow that had been ground into my face and stuffed inside my clothes. I had never felt so miserable, so overwhelmingly crushed, so alone.

At home that evening I made two dozen snowballs. I packed them harder than any I'd ever made before. Each one perfectly round, perfectly sized, marked for a Grade 4 kid. I placed them neatly in rows in a cardboard box and hid them in a dark corner of the basement. Sometime in the future, some warm summer day when there's no snow on the ground, those Grade 4 bullies won't even be thinking of snowballs. That's when I'll get even with them.

Several months went by before I went to retrieve my snowballs from their basement hiding place. At first I thought that my brother had stolen them. It was a while before it sunk in that my secret stash of snowballs had melted away.

---

[9] Today, "cowboys and indians" has unacceptable connotations. I use the term here because it was the vernacular of the time.

Backyard Snowfort — 1949
Our sense of "territory" probably began when we defended and attacked snowforts

In Grade 4, Donald Williams and I saw a movie about a tribe of pygmies in Africa who lived in grass huts and hunted with spears. They looked no bigger than us and appeared to be always happy. We thought we'd try being pygmies. So we built our own grass hut in a secluded corner of Mrs Turvey's orchard where the grass was long, and wild saplings could be hacked down and used for the hut's frame.

Construction was remarkably easy and the bunches of grass which we wove onto the exterior of the four-foot-high structure were so tight that when the woven grass door was closed no light could enter. The other kids in the neighbourhood joined in the fun and, before long, there were several grass huts scattered about the orchard.

We pretended we were pygmy hunters and attacked each other's huts, hurling spears made from sharpened garden stakes. We used garbage-can lids for shields. One day, my brother Johnny lowered his shield just as Donald flung a spear at him. Thwack — it hit Johnny in his face, just above his eye. There was a lot of blood and a lot of screaming. I felt sickened. Donald felt so bad he ran away and hid from the world for three hours. But luckily, Johnny's eye was saved.

Grass huts were our hangouts for a couple of summers. Two or three of us would gather inside, savouring the light from a candle and nibbling some booty raided from a neighbour's garden. I remember the time we returned from a garden raid to find that our pygmy hut had burned to the ground. Blaming an enemy war party rather than a neglected candle, we decided it was time to go underground. So we experimented with the ultimate in deception and camouflage — underground forts.

I dug three underground forts, one in a hidden corner of my back yard and two in the O'Malley's vacant lot. We built them by digging deep fox-holes, like graves in a cemetery, and covered them with boards and dirt, and disguised the top with leaves and grass. As fortresses, these underground hideouts were useless. How could you defend them when you were cooped up below ground? And once inside, there was no way to spread the camouflage over the trap-door.

But I do remember the thrill of spending an hour or two under-ground alone by myself on frosty autumn evenings, bundled up warm and toasty and lit by the flickering flame of a single candle. Little crawly things would skitter around my legs, and flying things would fizzle to a crisp in the flame of the candle, but I loved the earthy smells and the solitude, alone in my underground fort.

By the time I was twelve, our forts became more sophisticated. They had to withstand enemy attacks, mostly make-believe, but occasionally real. We took over a grove of tall cedars in the overgrown lot behind our property. Ten feet above the ground we built a fortress, using old boards pirated from neighbours' fences and woodsheds and abandoned chicken coops. Our cedar-tree fortress became an impregnable sanctuary. There was a retractable ladder and a hidden trap door — and a rope pendulum, high in a nearby tree, to simplify recapture if we were over-run by the enemy.

We defended our fort with cap-guns, water pistols and sling-shots. We trained with mock battles amongst ourselves, taking turns as attackers and defenders.

I remember a couple of fights where we actually faced a real enemy; a group of kids who lived on nearby Elm Street, whom we dubbed the Elm Street Gang. The first assault was prearranged — some friendly taunts back and forth across the road on the walk home from school. We rushed straight home to drop off our lunch buckets and call out reinforcements. Paul, Donald, Johnny and me, defending our fort against four Elm Street kids. The anticipation was almost unbearable. They charged our ramparts, screaming and yelling and hurling fir cones and chestnuts, just like the Indians in the movies attacking Fort Apache. Neither side ever admitted defeat.

Whenever we defended our forts against alien groups of kids, I felt I was participating in something noble and honourable. It was my duty to defend my neighbourhood. Sometimes I was afraid in these battles, but deep down I always knew that if I was ever in real danger, Donald would get us out. My best friend Donald was much bigger, and I was sure that he was invincible.

A week or two later we tried a surprise attack on the Elm Street Gang's tree fort. We didn't succeed, and in the following weeks found ourselves defending with more serious weaponry. We used buckets of water to repel invaders and even traded shots with stones fired from slingshots.

The slingshot was a weapon of last resort, for it was lethal. Our slingshots were carved from the forks of green-maple branches, to which we attached strips of rubber cut from an old inner tube, and a pouch cut from the hide of an old baseball. They'd fire a well-chosen stone with considerable accuracy and fearsome results.

One year, providence delivered to our neighbourhood the makings of a perfect fort. In November 1951 the Wollastons purchased a huge truckload of firewood. But it wasn't ordinary cordwood — it was rectangular chunks of rough fir, each weighing ten to twenty pounds. The chunks were perhaps a foot or two long, and of varying heights and widths. I think they were saw-mill scrap from the ends of huge beams.

This pile of firewood was a real-life set of building blocks that could be stacked and configured to make structures with unlimited possibilities. Johnny's diary contains dozens of references to our creative inventions over a period of four months.

First we piled the blocks to make a fortress, complete with turrets and a dungeon. Our imaginations had been fueled by pictures in the Classics Comics that we all read, such as *Prince Valiant*, *Joan of Arc* and *A Connecticut Yankee in King Arthur's Court*. We took turns playing the role of foreign armies, laying siege with rotten apples and braving the return volleys of chestnuts, as the defenders held out in our impenetrable fortress under attack from King Arthur and his Knights of the Round Table. The following week our woodblock fortress morphed into the great pyramid of Cheops, and we returned to its burial chambers in the dark of night, reading comics and "exploring" secret passages by candle light. Another time our blocks transformed into a submarine at a depth of twenty thousand leagues under the sea, as we accompanied Captain Nemo on the wondrous voyage of the *Nautilus*.

One foggy Saturday morning, our woodpile was an armoured cavalry tank. Jonathan was in the driver's compartment, Donald was feeding high-explosive ammunition from the magazine to the turret, and I was manning the fifty-calibre machine-gun. As I peered through the gun-sight, trying to spot the imaginary enemy, I could hear Paul in the engine room below, firing up the motors for battle.

A pea-soup fog lay thick and heavy all around. The acrid smell of burning autumn leaves intensified the reality of our impending combat. As I scanned the foggy gloom, the oppressive silence was broken only by the droplets falling from the wet trees onto the hard ground. Minutes before, we had heard enemy fire, and our nerves were taut, expecting to come under attack at any moment.

Suddenly we heard it again: the rat-a-tat-tat of a woodpecker boring for bugs in the trunk of a nearby tree. Wow, the drama of war! Oh, how I wished Paul could put life into our engines and propel us through the fence toward Elm Street, with Donald's high-explosive shells bursting from our turret gun as we charged into battle against the Elm Street Gang.

The last fort that I made was at Pasley Island, where I spent my summers from the age of nine to fifteen. The band of kids that I hung out with in the summer of 1952 built a huge structure on a cliff-top overlooking North Bay. We built it entirely from driftwood, and it was big enough to sleep all six of us. We slept in our fort several nights, swatting mosquitoes and swapping ghost stories. Lying in our sleeping bags, we kept one eye open for a possible attack from the kids whom we'd excluded from our group. The outcasts, who included my brother, were building a fort of their own at South Bay, so we had to keep watch. But they never attacked.

We had a special ceremony to initiate Mike Rankin's brother, Pinty, into our gang. We feasted on cookies and Kool-Aid and made him swear an oath of allegiance. Mike, who at fourteen was the oldest amongst us, made us prick our fingers with his jack-knife. Then we clasped each other's hands so our blood would mingle. Pinty repeated our solemn declaration that he'd obey the rules of our gang and never give away its secrets. It was the same blood oath that Tom Sawyer and Huck Finn made when they left home to raft down the Mississippi.

For me, it was intoxicating to participate in this ritual. I felt proud to be a member of such a close-knit club.

We knotted a thick rope around Pinty's ankles and looped the other end over the branch of a tree. Then we brothers-in-blood hoisted him slowly, feet first, until his head was off the ground. The rope cut into Pinty's ankles, but we told him we wouldn't let him down until he stopped snivelling. Eventually his screams were so loud that his mother heard the commotion.

She ran from their cottage and suddenly burst upon us from the woods.

I can't imagine what went through her mind when she came upon her son hanging by his heels, but I know what we gang members did. We let go of the rope and fled, barely hearing the thud as poor Pinty crumpled to the earth.

Pinty never did join our gang.

Our most memorable battle was a raid organized by our dads. In those days, parents seldom involved themselves in their children's play but, in August 1954, three fathers at Pasley Island organized a war game which pitted a raiding party of North Bay kids against some South Bay adversaries. Brigadier "Budge" Bell-Irving, who ten years before had commanded the Canadian forces that liberated Amsterdam, trained us North Bay kids. Another dad, Colonel Cec Merritt, who was awarded the Victoria Cross at Dieppe in 1942, was in charge of the South Bay squad.

The raid turned out to be a big deal, requiring serious training in warfare. Budge spent considerable time over two weekends instructing five of us North Bay kids how to travel noiselessly through the woods, how to cover each other when crossing open spaces and how to avoid making silhouettes against the skyline. We practiced the "leopard crawl" and learned to move in "diamond formation" with a "point-man" and a "tail-end-Charlie." I assume the South Bay boys received similar training.

The "operation" took place on a night when the moon was almost full. The five of us met after supper at Budge's house to be given our final briefing. The scenario, as it turned out, was that we were going out on a night reconnaissance, with the objective of capturing a map located in a cabin near South Bay. The cabin belonged to Brigadier General Rockingham who had just returned from commanding the Canadian Army in the Korean War. The adults (Maj. Bell-Irving, Col. Merritt and Brig. Rockingham) would be referees, walking the trails with lit cigarettes to identify themselves. Their job was to decide the outcome of encounters between opposing patrols in the dark.

This wasn't just an adult version of capture-the-flag — this was the real thing!

Budge helped us blacken our faces and hands with charcoal, and sent us off single file into the night, with Johnny in the lead and me as tail-end-Charlie. Accustomed as we were to moving around the Pasley Island trails in the dark of night, we didn't have flashlights. We advanced on a roundabout route, through half a mile of woods, steering clear of obvious approaches, keeping off the trails and trying to avoid dry twigs and crackly leaves on the forest floor.

An hour later we closed on the objective. I moved into action as the decoy. I was supposed to create a commotion on the enemy's flank while the rest of my patrol snuck up on the cabin. But I got lost in the darkness and stumbled deeper into the black woods. I thought I heard noises all around me — branches crackled, an owl hooted. Perhaps it was an enemy outpost! I was afraid. What if I broke a leg or starved to death before I was found.

Our side won. We captured our objective. But I didn't share in the glory. I just felt lucky that night to come out of the darkness alive.

The "Ruins of Ross" — 1953
Many of my childhood summers were spent at our cottage on Pasley Island

Chapter 8

The Ruins of Ross

When I was ten years old, my parents bought a piece of waterfront on Pasley Island. About a mile long and half as wide, Pasley is located between Bowen and Keats Islands in the mouth of Howe Sound. The island has no ferry or bridge linking it with Vancouver and, in those days, its location made access difficult, which gave Pasley a feeling of isolation. It was to become our summer camp for the remainder of my childhood.

Thirty families got together and bought the island in 1951. Dad selected a site on a point of land at the north end of the island and hired a carpenter, Mr Wibley, to build us a cabin. Our lumber was unloaded from a barge in June of that year and, by the time our family arrived for our summer vacation two weeks later, the cabin was almost complete. Johnny and I helped Mr. Wibley roll on the asphalt roofing while Mum painted the walls and floors.

From the start, Pasley developed a reputation as being a bit country-clubbish, somewhat elitist. The island attracted wealthy families who built expensive cottages with modern conveniences.

But our cabin was not grand. It was a rectangular box with a flat roof and big windows across its front. The big windows provided a spectacular view of Mt Garibaldi and the Lions, and the flat roof was greatly appreciated by the crows, who found it useful for opening clams and mussels which they dropped from the sky above. My first job when we opened up the cabin each summer was to shovel away the seafood cocktail which the crows had accumulated on our flat roof over the winter.

We spent six summers in our cabin at Pasley. We had no fireplace, no electricity, and no plumbing. In 1955, when my parents stopped spending their summers on the island, most other cottages had flush toilets, running water, propane stoves and fridges. But we Rosses were still drinking water from buckets, crapping in a one-holer and reading by candle light. At a Pasley Island shareholders' meeting in 1960, dinner was served on place-mats that featured a map of the island. The cottages were identified on the map by light-hearted labels. Ours was labelled the "Ruins of Ross."

On the island was a resident caretaker, Mr Boyd. Our first summer, Dad retained Mr Boyd to dig a well for us. He tromped around the woods behind our cabin, using a forked branch from a green willow tree, which he called a divining rod, to try to find an underground water source. When his divining rod twitched and pointed to the ground, he and his son, Stan, started digging.

A bunch of us kids watched as the two Boyds sweated in the hot sun, hour after hour, throwing shovelful after shovelful of heavy dirt out of the three-foot-square hole into which they were slowly disappearing. We were finally allowed to help when, at a depth of five or six feet, buckets and rope were required to remove the dirt. There were no backhoes or mechanical shovels or augers in those days.

At a depth of eight feet, the shovels encountered a layer of hard blue clay. Mr Boyd produced a box of dynamite, which all the old-timers used for blasting tree stumps and breaking up rocks. He showed us how to insert the little metal blasting caps into the sticks of dynamite. Then he climbed out of the hole, paying out a length of fuse behind him. He cut the fuse with his jack-knife and let us light it. We all took cover and waited for the whoompf — and then the shower of rocks and chunks of clay hitting the ground all around us. We repeated

The Chopping Block
Chopping firewood was one of our daily chores

the procedure several times before water suddenly bubbled up through the fractured clay.

We dug a privy — Dad and Johnny and I. No divining rod, no dynamite, no Mr Boyd and stalwart son to help us. And no soft ground around our cottage. Everywhere the bedrock was close to the surface, making digging impossible, so the privy ended up too near to the well. Our drinking water had a skunky taste, so Mum took a sample to the university for tests. It turned out that the water was not safe for drinking. For a while after that, we boiled it. Our parents treated it with whiskey. But eventually we just drank it straight from the well. We survived.

Our well had no pump. We dropped a bucket on a rope, carefully, so as not to knock the sides and disturb the dirt. There was a trick to dropping the bucket so that it would flip over and scoop the water, rather than float uselessly on top of it. It also took skill to avoid bringing up a dead mouse or a snake. And struggling along the uneven

The Garbage "Dump"
Getting rid of our daily garbage was a somewhat clandestine chore

trail back to the cabin with two full buckets of water each morning was a hundred yards of torture. Wire handles biting into flesh, arms stretched from their sockets, shins banged by buckets tipping their water into my shoes.

In those days all kids had daily chores which had to be completed before we could go off to play. Family roles were fairly well defined — mothers cooked and cleaned and ran the home, fathers worked in town all week and only showed up on weekends. Most kids spent an hour or so each day on routine chores ranging from filling the kerosene lamps and trimming their wicks to disposing of dead mice from the traps. Johnny and I took turns lighting the fire in the cast-iron wood stove before breakfast, and while one of us split the firewood and filled the wood-box for the day's cooking, the other went to the well for water.

Dumping the garbage was another chore. We couldn't let our garbage accumulate in plastic bags because plastic bags hadn't been invented, so garbage had to be disposed of daily. We simply dumped it in the ocean. All garbage was thrown into a cardboard box and rowed a few hundred yards from the shore and pitched overboard — uneaten food, bottles, tin cans, paper wrappers, grapefruit skins, everything. Later, most of it washed up on someone's beach, where the duration of its stay depended on the whim of the tides and the appetites of the seagulls and crabs. Some of us were more thoughtful than others, and we tried to sink the most objectionable items, more to prevent identification than to protect the environment.

During our summers at Pasley, there was no electricity and no portable generators. The only illumination at night was from kerosene lamps or candles or flashlights. The only way we could refrigerate food was by using ice, which had to be delivered all the way from Vancouver. The ice arrived three times a week, on the *Tymac* launch, wrapped in shredded newspapers and packed in cardboard cartons, each addressed to the family who had ordered it. When they left Vancouver, the blocks of ice weighed fifty pounds but, by the time they were dumped into our Pasley iceboxes, they were considerably lighter.

Most perishables were kept in meat safes, which were wire mesh containers placed in the shade somewhere out on the porch, or underneath it. They did little more than keep the flies and vermin away while the food rotted. Milk and butter were kept in small crocks (containers made of terracotta) which were cooled by water evaporating from their base. But despite these age-old methods of delaying the maggots, the rot and the mould, we learned as I'm sure our forefathers did, to eat rancid butter and mouldy cheese and powdered milk.

Fresh meat and vegetables were scarce. We ate a lot of canned foods. When we could, we lived off the land, enjoying the abundance of berries and oysters, clams and crabs. Fish were plentiful, and seldom were we skunked when we rowed to the hot fishing spots around the island. We caught and ate so many coho and spring salmon and rock cod that I learned to hate eating fish for the rest of my life.

Our groceries arrived three times a week from the Woodwards department store in Vancouver. They came on the tiny *Tymac* launch, which could turn the three-hour voyage from the city into an epic journey. The little vessel looked like a streetcar — half a dozen wood-framed windows along each side, with an interior of hard wooden seats separated by a long aisle. When the sea was rough, the *Tymac* pitched and rolled uncomfortably — and sometimes terrifyingly — as the salt spray crashed over her cabin. Stuffed inside, with the cabin full of boxes and parcels destined for isolated cabins in Howe Sound — with regular stops at Tunstall Bay on Bowen Island, North Bay on Pasley and Eastbourne on Keats Island — the passengers suffered claustrophobia along with the engine fumes and vibrations and seasickness.

"*Tymac* ahoy!" some sharp-eyed kid would bellow, as the little vessel hove into sight rounding Pilot Rock, the white wave at her bow like a bone in a dog's teeth. The *Tymac*'s arrival at Pasley each Tuesday, Thursday and Saturday morning was an eagerly awaited event that brought all the kids and dogs and most of the mothers to the dock at North Bay for a little gossip and a lot of confusion, as people tried to identify their groceries or their newly arrived guests. Mac, the ageless skipper with the wire-rimmed glasses, worked his way aft, passing the cartons of groceries out through the streetcar windows, and we kids would help Mr Boyd load them into waiting rowboats or lug them up the dock to his World War II jeep before the dogs had a chance to pee on the cartons. Then we'd scramble onto the jeep or its trailer and bounce along the rugged track through the forest, helping to deliver groceries to cottages across the island.

When the groceries were delivered and our chores were done, we disappeared into the woods or onto the water to spend the happiest days of our childhood.

In those days there were two horses on the island. They were named "Smokey" and "Star," and belonged to Penny Bell-Irving, one of the islanders. At first, Penny got us kids to help feed and groom her horses, for which we were rewarded with riding lessons. Because there was nowhere they could escape to, Smokey and Star just roamed freely wherever they liked, and before long we learned to catch them and ride them unsupervised. It was a sort of special pact that we worked

"Smokey" and "Star"
These two horses grazed at-large and eventually accepted us as passengers

out with Smokey and Star — they'd let us sit on them in the pasture in the middle of the island or in the orchard at North Bay, so long as we didn't interfere with their grazing. As time went on, we got bolder and Smokey and Star became more tolerant, until eventually some of us became quite good at bare-back riding.

Each summer we'd have more and more difficulty convincing Smokey and Star that their winter freedom was over, and cajoling them into letting us aboard. But their desperate escape strategies only made us better riders. Until the inevitable encounter with low-hanging branches.

Most days, when the weather was good, we'd swim and play on the beaches, building sand castles and race tracks for the small crabs we found in tidal pools and under rocks. When the tide was out, we'd dig for clams or gather oysters along the rocky shores which bordered most of the island. We'd mount day-long expeditions to explore the rugged shoreline around the more remote bays and headlands, searching for driftwood treasures while balancing on teetering logs that were stranded above the tide line by winter storms.

When we went out on the water we didn't bother to tell our parents and we didn't wear life jackets. Outboard motors and planing hulls had only just begun to replace the old wooden clinker-built boats with their reliable Briggs and Stratton inboard engines. Everyone learned to row a boat and paddle a canoe. We could circumnavigate the island in a rowboat in half a day, and we spent countless hours exploring the coastline in dinghies and kayaks, poking into coves and drifting over shoals and reefs, pretending submerged rocks were minefields or sunken galleons.

We built outrigger rafts by stabilizing a large buoyant log with a couple of struts extended to a smaller log, an idea I took from a movie I saw about the Polynesians. One memorable day we assembled a flotilla of six outrigger rafts and paddled together on an excursion to nearby Silver Island.

Several families owned small sailing dinghies. Molded fibreglass was the new rage for boat hulls, and before long there was a 9-foot Davidson dinghy on every wharf. Every kid learned to sail in these little boats and when the wind was right we had many impromptu sailing races.

My strongest memories of our summers at Pasley Island were the lazy hours we spent hanging out at the wharf in North Bay. The island kids would often assemble on the floats or in the boats moored alongside — row boats, sailing dinghies and clinker-built putt-putts — to gossip and wile away the time as we coiled and spliced ropes or whittled pieces of driftwood.

Hanging out on the North Bay wharf was the seashore equivalent of the hours we spent hanging out in the Macdonald Street trees. Maybe even better, because the seashore offered so many diversions. We tinkered with motors and pumped out oily bilges. We adjusted mooring lines, constantly perfecting our clove hitches, bowlines and reef knots. We fished for shiners over the sides of the floats and several times a week we conspired to throw some unfortunate victim into the water, usually fully clothed and always for the slimmest of reasons.

The wharf was the hub of all Pasley Island activity. In my early years at Pasley, very few islanders had their own float or moorage, so most visits to the island began and ended at the North Bay wharf. It was here that our summers commenced with such anticipation each June and ended with sadness as we returned to a new school year in September. And every Friday evening through the summer, families congregated on the wharf to greet the *Freemac* water taxi with its load of dads, tired from their week's work in the city. And every Sunday the ritual was repeated in reverse.

As we whiled away those idyllic summer days at the wharf, we were always alert for information about the local fishing. I have many memories of Budge Bell-Irving chugging to the wharf in his wooden-hulled, clinker-built *Pelican*, standing at the tiller in a blue turtle-neck sweater, his pipe dangling from his mouth, as he proudly displayed an eight-pound coho that he'd just caught off Whorlcombe Island. He'd throw us his mooring lines and we'd set his bumpers and tie *Pelican* to the wharf as only we experts could. Then there'd be a flurry of questions about where the fish were being caught and which lure was working best. Hootchie-cootchie? Or Tom Mack spoon with a herring dodger and six ounces of lead?

We did a lot of fishing ourselves. Right there — on the North Bay wharf. We spent hours on our knees leaning over the edge of the floats, fishing for shiners, small fish whose silver sides sparkled in the sun as they twisted and turned in their watery ballets beneath the float.

Catching a shiner didn't require much skill. Or equipment. You didn't need to go to the store for hooks or bait. It seemed that every time you sat down on the North Bay wharf you found yourself a hook — stuck in the seat of your pants. In fact, when you walked in bare feet across the rough-sawn planks of those weathered old floats you were just as likely to be stabbed by an abandoned fish hook as you were to be speared by a sliver. And for bait you didn't have to look any farther than the black mussel-shells which clung by the thousands from the underside of the floats.

"Let's have another fishing derby!" I suggested hopefully.

"Okay, what are the rules?" asked Graham, as he jerked a wriggling three-inch shiner up onto the dock.

"The biggest shiner wins!" Pinty replied.

"Whadya mean by biggest — longest or heaviest?" Johnny asked.

Pinty was bent over an opened mussel shell, extracting with his knife the black organ that we always thought was the heart. It's the best bait for shiners because, unlike the rest of a mussel's gooey innards, it is fairly solid and can be firmly impaled on the hook so that the fish can't easily tug it loose. "Gotta be the longest, not the heaviest," he said. "We got nothing to weigh 'em with. Length is easier — we just line 'em up, side by side, longest one wins."

Graham pulled another flapping fish onto the wharf. "When do we start?" he asked.

"Soon's I'm ready!" replied Pinty, his knife now busy working a splinter out of the bottom of his foot. "We need a time limit." Of course no one had a wrist watch — watches wouldn't survive a summer at Pasley because they weren't waterproof or shockproof in those days — so we agreed that the derby would end when a fish boat that we could see off the distant shore of Bowen Island passed out of sight behind Pilot Rock.

Everyone dropped their lines over the edge. On all sides of the float bodies bent over the water, bums in the air, heads barely clear of the wavelets lapping against the mussel-covered logs. Eyes stalking the underwater prey, arms jerking in response to the fishes' nibbles.

"Got one!" "Got another!" "Holy . . . , here's a huge one!" "Shit, I missed him!"

Scaly, silvery bodies were soon flapping along the deck. The contest was barely a few minutes old before it became obvious that many of the shiners were almost identical in size, and picking a clear winner was going to be difficult. So Graham, who seemed to be having the most luck, suggested, "Instead of the longest fish, let's say the winner is the guy who catches the most fish."

It was agreed. We'd start over. "Most fish caught before the white sailboat reaches the point of Mickey Island wins."

By now, the deck was covered in mussel shells, mussel guts, sea worms and dead shiners. Everyone fished furiously, cutting, baiting, jerking, unhooking, baiting again.

"Time's up!" shouted Pinty, as the white sails disappeared behind Mickey Island.

We counted our catches. Graham had nine, which was two more than anyone else.

"Graham's the winner," said Pinty. "Let's do it again."

"Wait a minute," protested Malcolm. "I've got more fish than he has." In his hands he held a particularly fat shiner which he'd lifted from the small pile at his feet. When he had our attention, he squeezed it gently. Out popped a baby fish, perfectly formed and quite alive! Then another and another and another.

"Eight, nine, ten, eleven," counted Malcolm, as he manipulated the pregnant mother into giving more births. Most species of fish lay eggs; but shiners, like the little sticklebacks that we netted back home in the sloughs at the foot of Macdonald Street, give birth to live babies.

The shiner derby ended in a fisheries research project, as we selected our fattest prizes and squirted each other with volleys of tiny fish, like pips squeezed from ripe cherries.

Then we gathered around Malcolm and threw him in the water.

*   *   *

In 1964 Malcolm bought the Ruins of Ross from my dad. He quickly tore down the "Ruins" and replaced it with an attractive modern cottage.

Fresh Bear Tracks in the Mud
Mum taught me to distinguish between Grizzly and Black Bear tracks

Chapter 9

Lore of the Broken Twig

When I was a youngster, I felt tuned in to nature. Spending as much time in the outdoors as we did in those days, it seemed natural to mark the passage of the seasons by the patterns of the environment.

In my childhood memories, the arrival of spring was heralded by the croaking of frogs at sundown from nearby ponds and ditches. And by the dawn chorus of robins outside my bedroom window, suddenly impatient as though the lengthening days weren't long enough for the business of finding mates and building nests and raising their families. Springtime brought the fragrance of the blossoms on the fruit trees in Mrs Turvey's orchard and the charm of lambs and new-born foals romping in the fields at the foot of Macdonald Street.

The butterfly harbinger of spring was always a mourning cloak. On a warm afternoon early in March I'd come upon the first butterfly of the year, a mourning cloak floating lazily on its yellow-bordered purple wings, back and forth over the sun-warmed glade beside our woodshed. I started collecting butterflies when I was six years old, catching them in the neighbours' gardens, chloroforming them, pressing their wings and mounting them on pins in wooden cigar boxes. Just as gardeners know when different plants will bloom, so I knew when the different species of butterflies would show up in our neighbourhood.[10]

Soon would come the tortoiseshells and red admirals, which Donald and I captured over the nettles in the O'Malley's vacant lot. In May I'd be stalking the ubiquitous cabbage whites as they took over our vegetable patch, and by the time I netted my first swallowtail each year, I knew summer had fully arrived. The regal yellow and black wings of the swallowtail were the centre pieces of my collections, dwarfing the other butterflies pinned in the cigar boxes with their wings out-stretched, like fleets of tiny glider-planes.

And when summer came, I remember the sweet aroma of fresh-mown hay on the farms below Macdonald Street, and the hum of insects in the flowers and the candy-like taste of fresh vegetables pulled from the warm earth of our back garden.

The chronology of nature could handle all but a few annual mile-stones — we needed the calendar on our kitchen wall to tell us when to hang our Christmas stockings, or when to expect end-of-term exams. But it wasn't until I saw the V's of migrating geese in the skies above our neighbourhood and heard gunfire from the marshes of the Fraser River that I knew autumn had really arrived. Walking to school those crisp mornings in the fall, we filled our pockets with chestnuts for games of conkers, and with acorns for ammunition for our slingshots. Playing outdoors in our back yard, we saw the squirrels stashing their winter supplies from our hazelnut and walnut trees. And the sweet smells of summer were replaced by the acrid tang of the autumn leaf fires smouldering in back yards and along the edges of Macdonald Street.

I knew it was December when the heavy fogs closed in, moody and oppressive, eerie and dripping, muffling all sound.[11] As we walked to school on foggy winter mornings, I loved the monotonous drone

---

[10] Urban development and pesticides like DDT have drastically reduced the numbers and species of butterflies in Vancouver since my childhood.

[11] Fogs were much denser in the days of coal and sawdust furnaces. In those days there were also many sawmills which burned off wood waste in "bee-hive burners." Water vapour condensed on the particles of soot which were released by the inefficient combustion, creating fog so thick that a passenger would often have to walk in front of the car so that the motorist could see where to drive.

Butterfly Hunter
In search of exotic up-country specimens to add to my collection

of the fog horns, warning invisible ships of unseen hazards. The weird double-tones from anonymous directions providing proof that life existed somewhere out there.

And by December we usually ran out of fresh fruit and vegetables. Like the squirrels, we had to rely on stores of dried and canned foods to get us through the rest of the winter.[12] And then the overwhelming silence of heavy winter snowfalls. And you knew that the snow was thawing when you heard the staccato clanging of tire chains on bare pavement.

Nature's cycle would always repeat itself and before long, winter was over and the frogs were croaking again in the ditches.

When kids play outdoors as much as we did, interaction with nature's critters is inevitable. I suppose that's why I collected butterflies.

---

[12] Families didn't have home freezers. Only a trickle of fresh produce was trucked in from warmer climates, and none was flown here by air.

The Tadpole Tubs
Watching tadpoles morph into frogs

By the time my collection contained every species of butterfly native to Macdonald Street our attention turned to other insects. Any time we came across a wasps' nest hanging in a tree, we used the opportunity to hone our throwing skills. And when our stones hit the target, we got some quality sprinting practice. On hot sunny days we examined ants with the aid of a magnifying glass, and watched with glee as they burned to a crisp. And in Mrs Turvey's orchard we held contests to see who could catch the most grasshoppers.

We brought home slimy globs of frogs' eggs from the sloughs at the foot of Macdonald Street and watched them morph into tadpoles in Mum's outdoor laundry tub. When the tadpoles sprouted legs and turned into frogs, we slipped them into our pockets and took them to school as presents for the girls. Snakes were another favourite. In the days before pesticides, garden snakes inhabited every urban lot, and we caught them by the dozen in the long grass of Mrs Turvey's orchard.

Each summer ended with a trip to the Pacific National Exhibition, from which we always came home with a green chameleon to add to our current collection of snakes and frogs. The chameleons were supposed to change colour to blend in with their background, but like many purchases from those slick hawkers at the PNE, it never seemed to work when you got them home. The chameleons came with tiny collars and chains from which they inevitably escaped, and for a few days we'd get glimpses of them on some window sill, snapping up the flies with their remarkably long tongues.

We also bought little painted turtles at the PNE. Turtles were fun, because they're like gyroscopes — they always know which direction they're heading. If you pick one up and put it down facing backwards, it simply turns around and gets back on its original course. But put one of those little painted turtles on a table top, and it will invariably walk right over the edge and fall on the floor. Nature never meant for turtles to be on table tops. The turtles I brought home from the PNE usually spent a day or two in our bath tub before being banished to Donald's aquarium, where they joined such exciting creatures as sticklebacks and oarsmen beetles from the sloughs on the flats.

Rodents and birds weren't safe from us either. The Williams boys spent a week every summer on their friend's farm on Vancouver Island, and always returned with some unfortunate captive — a wild bunny or field mouse, perhaps a pair of cedar wax wings or a couple of salamanders. Paul built the best of cages to house them and fed them the most scientifically-correct diets but, eventually, inevitably they all died. And then the neighbourhood kids would solemnly gather, not for a funeral but for the autopsy.

We'd watch in silent awe as Paul slit their little bodies open and poked through their innards, searching for the cause of death. But did it really require an autopsy to explain why they perished? I figured they simply died of broken hearts.

Their little corpses reminded me of the top floor of the museum where Mum sometimes took Johnny and me. In those days, the museum was housed in the Carnegie Centre at Main and Hastings Streets, now a community centre for the residents of the Downtown Eastside. I remember the spiral marble staircase winding around a tall totem pole as it took us to the natural history exhibit on the top floor.

There, we gaped into hundreds of glass cases and shelves full of stuffed animals and dried plants and feathers and furs. There was a huge collection of insects, all mounted on pins that were stuck through their little bodies — the inspiration for my own butterfly collection. Entering the macabre top floor of the museum, with its musty smells and dim lighting and dead creatures, felt like entering the House of Death.

However, it wasn't as unsettling as the wild animal show that sometimes came to town on the Zoo Train. When I was about ten years old, two or three train cars full of lions and tigers and grizzly bears occasionally parked on the railway siding by West Boulevard at 43rd Avenue, just a few blocks from our home. Together with the rest of the neighbourhood kids, I filed through those train cars, just inches away from the most ferocious man-eating beasts on the planet. I remember feeling so sad that those magnificent animals which should have been roaming the forests and plains were crammed into tiny cages, pacing and panting and rolling their eyes. Their spirits were broken. And watching them, so was mine.

Shorty Stevens felt so bad that he offered one of the tigers a lick from his ice-cream cone. I watched in horror as Shorty discovered a tiger's tongue is considerably longer than a chameleon's — he quickly withdrew his empty hand as the entire cone was sucked through the bars in one lightning-fast tiger-slurp.

*   *   *

As a kid I spent a lot of time spying on people. I often hid in our front hedge and watched strangers walking down the street, figuring out who they were and why they used our street. Or I'd hide in the top branches of the cedar tree in our front yard and put the neighbours under surveillance. If I was out in the yard and heard a nearby door slam, I might slip behind the nearest shrub and start shadowing some innocent victim.

Secretly observing the mundane movements of unsuspecting

people gave me a feeling of power. It felt good to know more about them than they knew about me.

At the age of eight or nine I was inspired by the exploits of "The Shadow," who was the hero of a nightly radio show. The Shadow had acquired the hypnotic power to cloud men's minds so they couldn't see him. Being a bit of a sleuth myself, I spent much of my childhood wishing that somehow I too could make myself invisible.

Staying out of sight was a valuable skill for many of our childhood activities. Like garden raids. All our neighbours had vegetable gardens, and on summer evenings we'd sneak into their gardens, using cover and stealth to steal their crops. Peas, fresh off the vine, or succulent carrots, pulled from the dark earth, beans, radishes — they all tasted like candy when pillaged from under a neighbour's window.

The games I enjoyed most as a child were those where the object was to be unseen and undetected. That was the essence of hide-and-seek and kick-the-can. Even better than hiding was sneaking up. Sneaking up requires skill and technique in disguising movement and stifling sounds. The best sneak-up game was capture-the-flag, which we played for countless hours in the long grass of Mrs Turvey's orchard or the woods in O'Malley's vacant lot, or the sand dunes and gorse on Mud Island at the foot of Blenheim Street.

Advancing quietly on scouting missions in the Old Hag's Woods, I learned that a broken branch or even a torn spider web across the trail could betray the passage of my enemies. I learned to distinguish which footprints were the freshest and how to determine our quarry's direction by reading the broken twigs and bent blades of grass.

We practised the doctrine of silence. My dad had a rule that no radios were allowed in his car — and the driver's window must always be open. Otherwise, how could an approaching siren or a policeman's whistle be heard? We kids had the same rule as we tried to travel noiselessly through the forest, avoiding dry twigs and brittle branches. No talking. No radios.

We froze at the slightest sound from the woods around us, as though our lives depended on deciphering every little chirp or swish or crackle that broke the silence. We listened for the twittering of the forest creatures. The urgent chattering of a red squirrel or the sudden quiet of croaking frogs meant the enemy could be near by.

Walking along the trails during our summers at Pasley, we spoke in hushed tones and kept an ear cocked for approaching voices. I thought we were so cool — traveling single-file Indian style, motioning each other with hand signals, to stop or proceed, or to quietly step off the trail and meld into the shadows. You never knew what opportunities might suddenly crop up — a chance encounter on the trail could develop into an hour of shadowing some unsuspecting member of the South Bay Gang or trailing a couple of heart-throb teen-age baby-sitters.

On the trails at night I seldom used flashlights, fearing that light beams would reveal more about me than about the path I was walking. On spotting the glare of an approaching flashlight, I'd quietly fade into the undergrowth and start eavesdropping.

When I was a kid I never left home without a jack-knife in my pocket. You never knew when you might need to cut a fishing pole or sharpen a green-willow stick for cooking hot dogs over a fire. Or just whittle aimlessly on a piece of wood. In the spring, when the sap was running, we carved whistles from young alder branches. We loosened the bark on a length of sapling and slipped it off like a sheath. Then we'd notch out a chamber and slide the cylinder of bark back over the opening. These woodland whistles produced strong clear notes — always different — until the bark inevitably dried and split and dropped off.

For some reason, at an early age I developed a subconscious sense of direction. Perhaps it was an awareness of the position of the sun, which for me was an object of worship in rainy Vancouver. Perhaps the imposing presence of the mountain backdrop on Vancouver's northern horizon acted as a constant reference. For whatever reason, I always knew which way I was facing. I learned to find north from the position of the Big Dipper and its pointer stars in the night sky; or during the day by pointing the hour hand of my wrist-watch toward the sun. And to this day, wherever I am, I always seem to be subtly aware of my orientation in the universe, like a turtle that returns to its original direction when you turn it around.

I was eight years old when Mum showed me the large footprints of a bear on a trail above Shuswap Lake. She pointed to the grooves in the mud in front of the toes and said that only the claws of a grizzly leave such an imprint. A black bear's imprint doesn't usually show its claws. I remembered Mum reading to me stories of animals by Ernest Thompson Seton. I recalled the story of Wahb, the powerful silver-tip grizzly who had twice been hit by hunters' bullets and who had lost a toe in a farmer's bear-trap. I examined the grizzly tracks carefully, hoping to find the imprint of a left hind paw with a missing claw.

Excited by the discovery of bear footprints, I wanted to learn more about animal tracks. The Vancouver *Province* newspaper carried a weekly feature called *Wood Lore*, featuring an outdoorsman named Mark Trail. From Mark Trail I learned to recognize the footprints of small animals and a host of birds. I became familiar with the cat-like imprint of the mink, bigger than the irregular tracks of the weasel. Or the raccoon's distinct finger-like footprints, distinguished from muskrats by the groove in the mud where the muskrat drags its tail.

It thrilled me to encounter the early morning tracks of wild animals on the muddy banks of the Fraser River or a snowy field on the McCleery farm — the tracks and spoor always told a story. Detective-like, I'd try to solve their riddle. Often the marks of several animals interacted in weird patterns, with running or jumping or dragging. A bunch of feathers or a splotch of blood might sometimes turn the riddle into a crime scene, and deciphering the clues could be so exciting. Phoebe the Pheasant murdered by Colonel Coyote in the corn field.

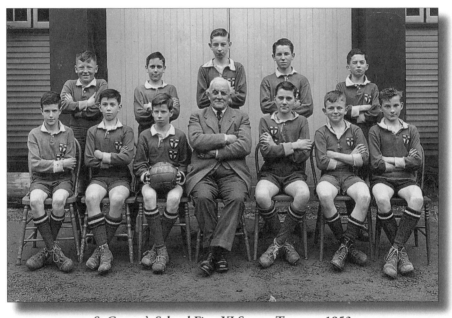

St George's School First XI Soccer Team — 1953
That's me claiming the ball

Chapter 10

The Right Stuff

My first four years of formal education were at Kerrisdale Elementary School on 41st Avenue at Carnarvon Street. I enjoyed school, and by the end of my fourth grade I was beginning to do reasonably well. I even got an academic award for topping my Grade 4 class. Then suddenly, for reasons that were apparent to neither my brother nor me, we were both sent off to private school.

I entered St George's School for Boys in September 1950. I would have been happier if I'd been sentenced to life in prison. My friends said that private school was for sissies, homos and spoilt rich kids. Little did I know how wrong they were.

I was a shy, awkward kid. I was very conscious of my skinny legs and large nose, and was uncomfortable in the company of girls. So for me, becoming a day-boy at St George's had one redeeming feature — there were no girls.

At that time, my dad was an elected member of the Vancouver Board of School Trustees. In fact, he was chairman of the School Board. So why were Johnny and I suddenly exiled to a dreaded private school? Years later Johnny suggested it was because our parents felt he wasn't reaching his potential at public school. And I was sent along with him so he wouldn't feel like he'd been singled out.

Nowadays, St George's is recognized as one of the leading schools in all of Canada. Its students consistently rank as British Columbia's very best in all activities from scholastics to sports. But when I was there, we didn't see ourselves as privileged. In those days private schools received no public funding and, during the eight years that I attended St George's, I came to feel that it was a second rate institution, with run-down facilities, a limited curriculum and under-paid teachers. I often pleaded with my parents to send me back to public school.

St George's School, at 3954 W 29th Avenue, had at one time been somebody's house. It was a jumble of gables and dormers and rickety fire escapes. And the rest of the campus was no better — a tangle of houses and sheds and add-ons that housed dormitories, dining rooms, classrooms, gymnasium and chapel.

For me, this was the beginning of eight years in a Dickensian atmosphere of duty prefects and house masters, Latin and Greek, and wooden desks scarred by a generation of schoolboys' initials. As a place of privilege and higher learning, St George's seemed a far cry beneath the ivy-covered red-brick government school that I'd left behind.

But the discipline and spartan conditions of private school were expected to build character. This I understood clearly as I entered Grade 5 that September.

It is said that the battles of the British Empire were won many years earlier on the playing fields of Eton. So it was that the playing fields of St George's were expected to build my character. Rugby was the school game, and every boy in the senior school was required to play "The Game." In those days, I felt that the success or failure of the school as a whole was measured by the outcome of the annual rugby games against Shawnigan Lake and University School on Vancouver Island.

I loved the autumn Saturdays when the whole school cheered wildly along the touch lines as the heroes of our First XV waged combat against the warriors from Shawnigan or University School. The walls of our gymnasium were adorned with large plaques that named the players of the school teams back to the beginning of time — back to

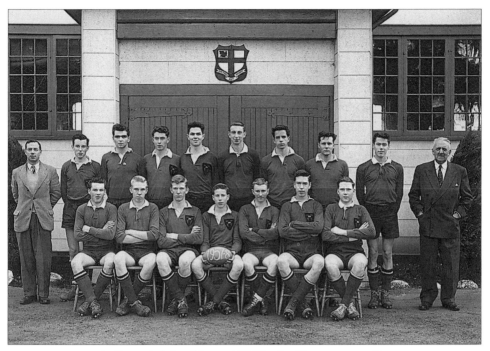

St George's School Second XV Rugby Team — 1957/58
That's me — Captain "Runt" Ross — with the ball

1931, the first year of St George's. When the student body assembled in the gym each morning for roll call, I'd gaze in awe at those neatly scribed names, the rosters of the school's heroes. Palmer, the Chambers brothers, the Tynans, Stubbs — the names were legendary.

Rugby was supposed to make us men. It was gritty — and yet polished; it was rugged — but with a touch of class. Rugby was harsh and uncompromising, a hard struggle that brought out the best in us. At the end of my first term in the senior school, the report card that I took home for my parents to sign contained a terse comment from the headmaster: "A promising rugger boy."

I was always the smallest in my class — Runt Ross they called me at school — but I loved sports and managed to hold my own on the rugby pitch. I had heart and savvy and quick hands. I played on each of the intermediate teams, but I was never a regular on the school's First XV, where runts would only be a liability.

In my final year I captained the Second XV to an undefeated 9 and 0 season. Team captains at St George's had many duties — in addition to being responsible for the conduct of our players on and off the field, we captains had to ensure that oranges were provided at half-time for the other team and that the visiting players got to shower first, before the hot water ran out. As captain, I was expected to write thank-you letters to the headmasters of the Vancouver Island schools after away games, knowing that my letters would be posted on their bulletin board, earning such endearing tags as "Who's that suckhole?"

It was all part of the character-building.

Like rugby players everywhere, I grew accustomed to dislocated fingers, swollen knees and sprained ankles. For me, each injury became a sort of red badge of courage,[13] a reminder that I'd played hard and given my best. For the rest of my life, soreness in my joints and limbs evoked in me warm pleasant feelings — reminders of the rewards for working or playing hard.

Rugby readied me for the battlefields of the British Empire.

In those days, St George's also tried to make us cricketers. It was an uphill battle because Vancouver kids weren't born with cricket in their genes. Kids with any ball skills had already spent too many school recesses playing scrub on a baseball diamond. Nonetheless, the school's English traditions endured, and each spring every one of us had to take our lumps on the cricket pitch.

In two of my intermediate years I travelled with the cricket team on the May long weekend to Vernon, where we played against Vernon Prep School. I have fond memories of their cricket pitch nestled between orchards, surrounded by apple trees in blossom, and hillsides speckled with yellow sunflowers. Between innings we'd break for tea on the veranda of the cricket pavilion, sheltered from the sun by a grove of huge cottonwood trees. I remember sipping my tea, which was served from silver teapots in china cups in this most English of settings, and being bewildered by an incongruous sign on the pavilion's

---

[13] From the American Civil War novel *The Red Badge of Courage* by Stephen Crane.

88

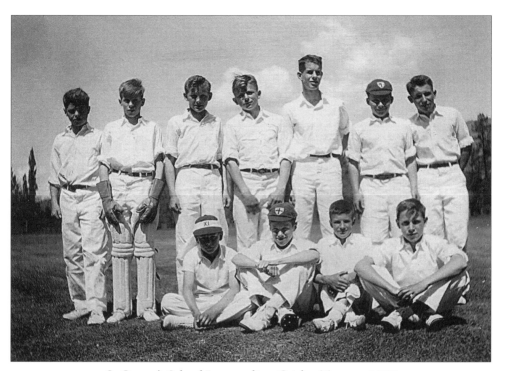

St George's School Intermediate Cricket Team — 1955
That's me (second from left) *wearing the wicket keeper's pads*

door. Carved in gothic script were the unmistakably German words, 𝔉𝔯𝔢𝔦𝔥𝔢𝔦𝔱 𝔇𝔲𝔯𝔠𝔥 𝔄𝔯𝔟𝔢𝔦𝔱. No one could explain this bizarre sign to me, but years later I learned its meaning — "freedom through work." I never understood the connection with cricket, but I discovered later that, during the First World War, the nearby army camp had housed German prisoners. For some reason the Prep School had acquired the sign when the Germans left.

For me, playing cricket dispelled the myth that it's a sissy's game. Cricketers appear to stand idly for hours in fields of clover, occasionally clapping applause or calling out inane comments like "Play up, there's a good chap." Their apparel looks more appropriate for the Queen's garden party — white shirts, long white trousers and white boots. Unlike baseball players, they don't even use a glove to catch the ball. But I soon found that it takes considerable courage to catch a well-hit cricket ball in your bare hand.

In my Grade 10 literature class I had to memorize a poem by Sir Henry Newbolt, called "Vitae Lampada" (The Torch of Life). Only a cricketer understands the opening lines, but for me, this poem epitomizes the St George's School of my time:

> *There's a breathless hush in the Close[14] tonight —*
> *Ten to make and the match to win —*
> *A bumping pitch and a blinding light,*
> *An hour to play and the last man in.[15]*
> *And it's not for the sake of a ribboned coat,[16]*
> *Or the selfish hope of a season's fame,*
> *But his Captain's hand on his shoulder smote*
> *"Play up! play up! and play the Game!"*

St George's, like all private schools, was divided into houses. I belonged to Tupper House, while Johnny wore the black shirt of the MacDougalls. In each sporting activity at all levels of the school the red-shirted Tuppers competed against the MacDougalls, a rivalry which ensured that every student participated, no matter what his skill level or interest. I particularly remember the cross-country runs. On the afternoons when our presence wasn't required on the rugby or cricket pitch, all students had to run through the trails of the University Woods. These runs culminated with the junior, intermediate and senior house runs, which were held at the end of each term, with points awarded to the winning house.

I was a reasonably good cross-country runner, and have fond memories of finally emerging from the woods at the end of an exhausting three- or five-mile race, and charging to the finish line

---

[14] English school playground.

[15] The last batter is up, and in order to win the game he must score ten runs, a task made more difficult because the setting sun is in his eyes and the rough ground causes the ball to bounce unpredictably.

[16] Exemplary performance on the cricket pitch is rewarded by ribbons attached to the players' coats.

on 29th Avenue in front of the old school. The last 200 yards were lined on both sides by schoolboys, each cheering madly for his particular house. My lungs were bursting, but exhilarated by the roar of my housemates, I'd give a final spurt, passing black shirts one by one. Each one passed, another point for Tuppers.

During my first couple of years at the school we were taught the manly art of boxing, another corner-stone of character-building. In fact, boxing matches were sometimes arranged to settle disputes. I have a strong memory of one such match that turned into a disaster.

Following a schoolyard bullying incident, the duty master decided the bully should be given a lesson in fair play. A few days later at morning assembly the headmaster ("The Beak," as we called him) gave a short lecture on bullying and proclaimed that cowardly behaviour would not be tolerated. The bully, a Grade 7 boy whom most of us were afraid of, was to be put in the ring against a gentleman, a boxer who could look after himself. The gentleman who would represent the forces of justice was a younger and smaller Grade 5 boy who was well-known to be a skilful boxer.

At lunch hour a boxing ring was measured up and traced in the schoolyard dirt. Eighty boys from Grade 4 to Grade 7 squeezed onto the tumbling mats spread around its sides. While the gloves were being laced, the duty master went over the Marquis of Queensbury rules. We'd all heard The Beak's message that the force of Good would overcome the force of Evil: however the difference between the fighters was ominous. The Grade 5 kid was a fancy little boxer with speed and finesse, but he looked intimidated by the extra 20 pounds and cocky air of the bully, who was strutting about with the confidence of some-one who's used to getting his way.

It was all over before the end of the first round. The villain simply overpowered the hero. He cornered him and crushed him with a flurry of punches so fast and violent that the little kid was swept off his feet. I can still see the tears rolling down the kid's blood-reddening face as the referee stopped the fight. Tears not because he'd been walloped. It was worse — he'd let the side down.

I'm sure there was a lesson there. It just wasn't what The Beak intended. We all admired the younger kid's pluck — he didn't have a chance, but he played The Game.

That courage in the face of overwhelming adversity was reflected by the second verse of "Vitae Lampada":

> The sand of the desert is sodden red —
>> Red with the wreck of a square that broke: —
> The Gatling's jammed and the colonel dead,
>> And the regiment blind with dust and smoke.
> The river of death has brimmed his banks,
>> And England's far, and Honour a name,
> But the voice of a schoolboy rallies the ranks,
>> "Play up! Play up! and play the Game!"

The school chapel was another arena for developing character. Every morning, five days a week, the entire school body (except for the half-dozen Catholics) attended chapel. It was an opportunity to learn that we are part of something greater than ourselves. But for me at least, those twenty-minute services were a mind-numbing waste of the chaplain's time. My years at St George's could be measured by the number of times my initials were carved into the wooden pews or the number of spit wads shot through paper drinking straws that remained stuck to the chapel ceiling.

Another area where St George's shone in those days was discipline. The school was known for its tough no-nonsense approach to misbehaviour and bad manners. While it's true that some boys were sent to St George's because their parents wanted them to experience the enriched quest for knowledge and the respect for authority that they thought would be instilled by the old English system of private schooling, the majority of my classmates were either misfits, discipline problems or slow learners.

To meet the challenges of controlling this potentially rebellious crowd of ruffians, a wide range of punitive measures was available.

To begin with, there was the uniform. At St George's, everyone was required to wear the school uniform — white shirt and school tie, grey trousers and navy blue blazer, shoes polished and shirt-tails tucked in. The uniform gave us a sense of identity, a subtle reminder that to misbehave while in the school's colours was to let the whole school down.

At the other end of the scale, major misdemeanours were punished by the cane. Nowadays, a society that doesn't let parents spank their children considers corporal punishment at school to be an act of barbarity. But back then we didn't think the practice of caning to be inappropriate. The cane was something we all feared. It hurt like hell. It was a punishment that we usually felt we didn't deserve. But we didn't question the system.

I'll never forget my first caning at St George's. My house master, Captain Robinson, was teaching literature to my Grade 5 class. "Cappy," as we called him, had a steel plate in his head from a war injury, and was prone to bouts of rage. It was my own fault that I didn't see this one coming — his jaw jutting forward, the stem of his rosewood pipe clenched between his teeth, pipe smoke curling past his one good eye. I should have known what was coming even before he hurled his chalk brush at me. I turned to acknowledge my classmates' snickers — and Cappy caught me.

"Ross II, see me in the masters' common room after school!"

At 3 o'clock as instructed I was waiting outside the masters' common room. Above the door I read the familiar words of the school motto — *Sine timore aut favore*. Without fear or favour. I knew the words, but I didn't really understand what they meant.

The waiting was almost worse than the punishment. Cappy answered my knock. "Uh, yes . . . Ross II . . . let me see now . . . you're here to be caned, aren't you? . . . Very good . . . come along in."

Did he say caned? What? The guilty verdict without even the benefit of a trial!

I entered the study hesitantly. How cosy it looks in here, I thought. The overstuffed chairs and sofas, the shelves full of books, the fireplace neatly laid with kindling ready to be lit. The little mementos on the mantle, photographs of school teams, a cricket bat in the corner, the large oak desk overflowing with papers.

Cappy selected a rattan cane from two or three leaning against the wall. I began to tremble. "This is going to hurt me more than it'll hurt you," he said as he motioned for me to lean over an armchair, spread-eagled from the back.

As each stroke found its mark, I wanted to scream, but the code of the caned doesn't allow any show of weakness. Stiff upper lip, and all that. As I gingerly straightened up after the third blow, I blurted out an involuntary "Thank you, sir." and hurriedly left the room before the tears would be noticed welling in my eyes.

Later, in the classroom, I showed off the three red welts across my bum to my admiring classmates. I'd earned a red badge of courage. Play up! play up! and play the Game!

When my brother entered Grade 12, they made him "head boy." It was a huge honour for Johnny. He'd been sent to St George's because it was feared that he wasn't reaching his potential — and then, finally, he was the captain of the school!

At the time, I didn't give my brother much credit for his achievement. He and I were very competitive, and I suppose I was more concerned about my own accomplishments than his. I figured the best thing about Johnny becoming head boy was that his position required him to board at the school, which meant I'd have Mum's cooking all to myself. Now that he was out of the house, I remember worrying how his head boy appointment might affect me at school. Like, how embarrassed I'd be if he screwed up. Or even worse, if *I* screwed up. I never dreamed he'd get to inflict punishment on *me*.

One of the duties of the head boy was to mete out punishment for minor infractions, such as rough-housing between classes or breaking the silence before grace at lunch. A first offence drew only a warning, but for a second infraction you were caned by the head boy. Even if you were his brother, apparently!

It happened that a senior prefect, a friend of my brother, caught me whispering in chapel. Only a few days earlier another prefect had given me a warning for attending assembly with my shoes not polished. Two infractions in one month meant a caning. So the school had a dilemma. Is it OK for a boy to be caned by his brother?

The Beak made a ruling and, at morning recess a week later, the prefects vacated their common room, leaving one behind to witness Ross I hit Ross II three times across the buttocks with a wooden rod.

Head Boy Johnny did not hold back for his younger brother. His face looked grim as he instructed me to stretch my arms over the stuffed armchair. I said nothing. It was clear that we both felt the injustice of the situation. But Johnny did not falter. He took the usual two step run-up and whacked my bum with every ounce of strength that his coiled body could deliver through rotating shoulders and flailing arm. As I felt the searing pain of each stroke, I wondered if Johnny was getting even for some long-forgotten injustice inflicted by his younger brother.

Unlike Cappy's or The Beak's canings, I don't think it hurt Johnny as much as it hurt me. Johnny never got to see the angry red welts that I unveiled to curious classmates an hour later. As far as I know, the caning didn't create any unresolved issues between my brother and me. Neither of us embarrassed the other. No hard feelings. Could there be a better example of the school motto than the sanctioning of the caning of one brother by another? *Sine timore aut favour*. Finally those words made sense to me.

My best achievements at St George's were in the classroom, where I did well because I loved to learn. I suspect that I was a horrid little know-it-all, and I'm grateful that I wasn't often bullied for being the nerd that I was, but I found it so empowering to acquire knowledge.

One of the reasons for my academic success was that scholastic skill is measured by scores on exams, rather than by ability to solve problems. To do well on exams, all that was required was to memorize, memorize, memorize. I spent literally hours every evening pacing back and forth in my bedroom, memorizing equations and charts and tables, or reciting my flash cards on the day's classes or chanting poetry in iambic pentameter.

Mum had always taught me to pay attention to details, so I learned my lessons by rote. By the time I graduated from St George's I could recite everything from the kings and queens of England to the periodic table of the elements. But do you think I could figure out how many trains you'd observe if you left Kings Cross at 8 am traveling at 60 mph, while oncoming trains left a terminus 100 miles away at half-hour intervals, coming toward you at 80 mph? The difficulty was that I wasn't learning how to think.

To become proficient at conjugating verbs in Latin or memorizing the world's capitals took time. So much time that even in the junior grades I'd have to begin committing my studies to memory at least two weeks before end-of-term exams. On the final three weekends before the end-of-terms in my senior years I studied up to ten hours a day. Sometimes it was difficult to fit all my duties into a normal day — prepping for exams, completing assigned homework, household and garden chores, polishing shoes and preparing my uniform for weekly cadet parades. But when I sat down to write an exam I could squawk the answers like a parrot — be it geometric formulae, obscure dates in English history or the precise punctuation in a passage from Shakespeare.

The final exam in Greek 92 was a case in point. Classical Greek is an exceedingly difficult language. Because I learned by rote, the strange Greek alphabet was the easy part. What *did* give me difficulty were the complicated Greek verbs with their three voices, four moods and seven tenses. And no easier were the three genders, three numbers (singular, dual and plural) and three declensions of Greek nouns.

The provincial matriculation examination for students of classical Greek, which I wrote at the end of my tenth grade, required that I construe a passage from *Xenophon's Anabasis*. The *Anabasis* (Αναβασισ Ξενοφου), a book of 42 chapters written entirely in Greek with no English translation, tells the detailed story of the retreat of a Greek army after its defeat in Persia. My skills at translating Greek were not up to snuff, and my only hope for passing the exam was to memorize the *Anabasis*. But without enough time to translate and memorize the entire book, I took a chance and guessed which chapter was most likely to be on the exam. My brother translated that chapter into English for me and I memorized his translation. ου πολλα αλλα πολυ.[17]

The gamble paid off, and when I graduated from St George's two years later, in 1958, the transcript of my matriculation results would record that the highest mark I achieved in all eleven of my university entrance examinations was in classical Greek.

I never failed an exam at St George's. I won the scholarship trophy in my final year, but as I progressed through university I discovered that it is not possible to memorize everything. As my studies got tougher and it became necessary to think for myself, I sometimes came up short. I appreciate the grounding St George's gave me in academics and athletics, but regret that I didn't try harder to be a creative thinker. I failed several courses at University, and the farther I progressed the more supplementals I was required to write.

However I did profit from learning to play The Game.

And today, over half a century later, I still remember the words of the poet:

This is the word that year by year
*   While in her place the School is set*
Every one of its sons must hear,
*   And none that hears it dare forget.*
This they all with a joyful mind
*   Bear through life like a torch in flame,*
And, falling, fling to the host behind —
*   Play up! play up! and play the Game!*

---

[17] Not quantity but quality.

Chicken-Run Athletes
The chicken-run in our backyard was our sport multiplex
(Note hurdle in background)

Chapter 11

Shirts vs Skins

Throughout my life I've had an enduring passion for sports. As a kid I lived for athletics, competing in one sporting activity or another almost every day of my childhood, and often several different sports a day.

As I shed my diapers, those endless wrestling and shoving fights of brotherly adversity evolved into more structured contests of backyard sprinting and jumping and kicking and throwing. The neighbourhood kids joined the fray, and scarcely a day would go by when our yard or the street out front wasn't a stadium for some sport that involved a ball and something to whack it with. For hours on end we competed in everything from flag football and field hockey to mini-golf and half a dozen forms of baseball. The skills acquired in those neighbourhood championships we honed on school playgrounds at recess and lunch time, and our collective talents were eventually harnessed for combat against other schools.

I represented my junior school in field hockey and soccer, and my senior school in rugby and cricket, but it would be a wild exaggeration to say that I excelled at any sport. At university I earned my intra-mural colours with hard-fought but unspectacular performances in touch football, basketball, soccer and lacrosse. And in the years that followed I played every sport in the western world with the exception of handball, hurling and jai alai. By the time I finally retired from combat and hung up my armour, I had become an enthusiastic jack-of-all-sports but a master of none.

I can clearly remember the way it all started. A bunch of us neighbourhood kids were hanging about the Williams' yard across the street, down on our hands and knees helping Dr Williams weed his front lawn. It was the spring of 1948, and I was seven years old. When the weeding became tedious, the eldest Williams boy, John, who would have been about thirteen, suggested we play baseball instead. Most of us didn't know anything about baseball, except that it sounded more fun than pulling weeds, so we jumped at the opportunity.

At the back of my yard, behind the old chicken coop, was a disused clay tennis court that hadn't seen a tennis match during my lifetime. We'd used it as a chicken run during the war, and the chicken manure had sprouted a tangled growth of long grass. It was surrounded by a twelve-foot high chicken wire fence that, according to John, would make an ideal baseball stadium.

John organized us into a work party and put us to work clearing base paths at one end of the old tennis court. We hacked away with scythe and sickle and, by lunch time, we had a path cleared through the long grass from what John called home plate to first base and on to second base. Then John sat us down and explained the purpose of the bases and the base paths. He described the positions — and we all wanted to be the pitcher. Then he explained the role of the batter — and we all wanted to be batters.

The neat thing was that this whole process of building our own baseball diamond and learning the positions before we could even hit a baseball gave me a real sense of ownership of the game. The best thing was that our parents weren't involved. In fact, parents never showed up to watch any of our sports, even when we played for our school. It was good enough that they knew how much enjoyment we got out of playing, and beyond that and laundering our kit, we didn't need any support or encouragement from them.

In the years that followed, the chicken-run stadium became the centre of our neighbourhood sporting universe. It was the perfect sports field, smooth and level and well-drained. Johnny and I were the groundskeepers and, for years, we pushed Dad's old Pennsylvania hand-mower back and forth, keeping the grass as neatly manicured as Yankee Stadium's infield. Eventually, the twelve-foot fences could no longer contain our fly balls, and our spaniel, Tommy, tired of pursuing those that had been hit over the fences into the neighbours' yards.

When I was eleven years old, we embedded a couple of posts at one end of our stadium and added a sturdy cross bar to make a mini-soccer goal. For years the neighbourhood kids took turns attacking and defending that goal in endless soccer games of three-and-you're-in.

The year that I turned twelve, Johnny and I equipped the chicken-run stadium with a high jump and hurdles. Track and field were not my strengths, but I was determined to win at least one event at the upcoming school sports day. We measured the correct height and spacing of a couple of hurdles and refined our technique with hours of sprinting and take-offs. We recorded precisely the heights of our daily high jump competitions. And when sports day came, to everyone's surprise I won the Junior Challenge Trophy, with a first in the hurdles and the 440 yards, and second place in the high jump.

Johnny and I were so competitive that everything we did turned into a life or death competition. And Johnny was secretly keeping score. Today, when I scan his diaries, it's like reading the sports pages of a daily newspaper. Here are some of his entries for July 1954 (he was fourteen and I was thirteen):

July '54
  Played golf & beat Bob 81 to 64 (18 holes).
  Played bike polo. Blue Spruce 20, Silver Salmon 15
    (I scored 8 of our 15).
  Played mark with Bob, Donald and Michael Brett.
    Score, Brett & me 6, D & B 7
  Played scrabble and beat Bob 296 to 215.

Played baseball. My team beat Bob's 9-8.
Played skip, in which Bob first (40), me second (33)
    Donald third (29) Elsie fourth (26), Patience fifth (24).
Had a family relay and I beat Bob for first time in my life.
Beat Bob at French Cricket 2/1, 4/5, 4/1.
Beat Bob in 200 yd dash.
I made new neighbourhood record in swing jump:17 ft ¼ in.

And that's just for one month. Imagine a whole childhood of Johnny's months, each one a balance sheet of wins and losses against his baby brother. Myself, I didn't keep a diary, but I remember how important those games were, and the euphoria of my own victories and the agony of my defeats.

This rivalry wasn't confined to the Ross siblings — it extended across the street to include the Williams boys. For several years, whenever Johnny and I found ourselves in a competition with the Williams brothers, we younger siblings always aligned ourselves together against our older brothers. Donald and I called ourselves the *Blue Spruce*, while Paul and Johnny were the *Silver Salmon*, and seldom in five years did the *Blue Spruce* lose to the *Silver Salmon*. The bike polo contest mentioned in Johnny's diary, above, being a notable exception. I marvel now at the names we chose for our teams. Why weren't we *Warriors* or *Bombers* or *Dragons*? I suppose society wasn't yet addicted to big-league sports culture, so our earthy choices reflected the values of our little neighbourhood group.

In our basement was a windowless room we seldom entered. It was dark and musty and smelled of moth balls. When we pulled on the string, which dangled from the ceiling, a naked light bulb would reveal dozens of old steamer trunks full of my ancestors' things. In these trunks we found a curious assortment of sporting apparatus; like polo mallets and croquet sets and badminton racquets in wooden presses. There were wonky wooden balls for lawn bowling, and a skinny canvass golf bag full of hickory-shafted clubs with names like mashie and niblick stamped on their blades. And in the farthest corner, tangled up with an old tennis net and hidden between rubber hip waders and a rusted Damascus shotgun, stood a pair of wooden-edged skis with cable harnesses. There were even swords with rapier-thin blades and helmets with wire-mesh visors that turned out to belong to my cousin, John Loewen, who had learned the art of fencing at school in England. It was like a collection of artefacts from the arenas of some ancient civilization.

The unique combination of the chicken-run stadium and our basement dark room produced some weird competitions. When the *Blue Spruce* tired of beating the *Silver Salmon* in football or grasshockey or the myriad variations of baseball (scrub or American ping-pong or 500 or French cricket), Donald and I would challenge our brothers to championship contests of lawn bowls or bicycle polo or back-yard golf.

Playing with this antique equipment gave me a curiosity for obscure sports. I'd often peer through the hedge at the Kerrisdale Lawn Bowling Club and listen to the old folks dressed in white, to pick up on their terminology and rules. Then I'd drag a bag of bowls out of our dark room and see how far I could make them curl on our moss-covered lawn. And I remember weekend afternoons sitting on the fence at the Southlands Riding Club, a short walk down Macdonald Street from our home, watching the bumping and checking of sweating ponies as they charged up and down the polo field in thundering polo matches. And the clash of the mallets inspired us to rush home to our chicken-run stadium and dark-room polo mallets and mount our bikes for a chukker[18] or two of our own.

When I was twelve I watched my cousin John compete in fencing tournaments[19] at the University of British Columbia, and I brought home the tactics of sword play. Those rapier-thin swords in the basement dark room soon replaced garden stakes in our neighbourhood swordplay, and sometimes we donned the wire mesh helmets and padded jackets, and lunged and feinted with foil and sabre.

---

[18] A chukker is one of the six periods into which a polo match is divided.
[19] Fencing is one of only four sports featured at every modern (since 1896) Olympics.

Some sports just didn't belong in the chicken-run stadium. One of these was ice hockey. Unlike the rest of Canada, where ponds and lakes stay frozen for half the year, ice hockey wasn't bred into the DNA of Vancouver kids. Before the Kerrisdale Arena was built in 1949 there was only one artificial ice rink in the entire Lower Mainland. But fortunately, we had a couple of cold spells in the late 1940s which froze the Wollaston's fish pond and gave our neighbourhood a chance to try skating.

In the early 1950s we had four cold winters which froze the ponds and sloughs on the McCleery farm at the foot of Macdonald Street, and the neighbourhood gang shouldered our skates and hockey sticks and trooped down the hill to find our own private patch of ice. Sometimes we were the first ones there — no tracks but our own. The ice was so fresh and transparent that we could see the reeds in the water below.

We played hockey from dawn to dusk, stopping only for hot chocolate and a mid-day wiener roast. We ignored the numbness and pain of squeezing into skates several sizes too small — the infrequent spells of cold weather seldom justified buying skates that would keep up with the growth of our feet. Although tube skates were becoming fashionable, I struggled along on a pair of Hans Brinkers that I found hanging by their knotted laces on the wall in the basement dark room.

There was no sport that I ever enjoyed more than ice hockey. Anyone who has experienced the exhilaration of a day of outdoor shinny will know how hard it is to acknowledge that the day must end. No matter how your aching lungs protest, you take one more end-to-end twilight rush. And then just one more. And then one more after that. And then another . . . . Long past the point of exhaustion, we'd finally yield to the night and trudge on blistered feet back up the hill to our disinterested parents.

When there was no ice, we played roller-skate hockey on the Johnson's driveway. Mr and Mrs Johnson, the elderly couple who lived next door, were either very kind or very deaf, for they never complained about the cacophony of balls slamming against their garage door, the bickering, the cheering, and worst of all the deafening clatter of the roller-skates themselves. If you haven't skated over rough asphalt on side-by-side steel wheels strapped to your Buster Brown scampers, then you don't know what vibration really is. Bone-shaking, ankle-wobbling, ear-splitting hell on wheels — but oh, such a great feeling when you deek around the defenceman and snap a wrist shot over the goalie's shoulder, thwap against the Johnson's garage door!

As a child, my interest in sports wasn't confined to the playing field. I discovered that I could be happy as a spectator. Like rugby, for instance. St. George's School took bus loads of aspiring young players to Brocton Oval to watch the world's best play rugby. I remember cheering wildly from the sidelines as the British Columbia Reps lost to a succession of international rugby teams passing through Vancouver on their way to, or from, Down Under. Like lion cubs learning from their parents how to stalk and tackle prey for dinner, we school boys were supposed to learn from watching the famous *Barbarians*, the *Springboks*, the *Wallabies* and the mighty New Zealand *All-Blacks*. Standing close along the sidelines, I was amazed at the ferocity and power in those international rugby line-outs and scrums.

On my twelfth birthday, Dad took me to the Forum at the exhibition grounds to watch my first hockey game: the Vancouver *Canucks* lost to the New Westminster *Royals*. I remember being surprised at the speed of the game and frightened by all the fighting on the ice. The game had more personality in those days — goalies didn't wear masks, players didn't have helmets, and there was no glass between players and the fans. And between periods, instead of Zambonis, the ice was resurfaced by a squad of smooth-skating rink rats.

In the BC *Lions'* inaugural season — the *Lions* Roar in '54 — dad took me to Empire Stadium to see my first football game. I'd played a lot of touch football, but never seen the real thing. And when By Bailey plunged over the goal line from 3 yards out, I witnessed the *Lions'* first ever touchdown. Well, maybe I didn't see it — I hadn't yet got the hang of where to watch when the ball was snapped.

Every autumn, major league baseball stole an inordinate share of our attention. For two weeks in October, at World Series time, school boys who, for the rest of the year knew nothing about the big leagues, suddenly became die-hard *Dodgers* or rabid *Yankee* fans. Myself, I loved the *Yankees*, and only once in ten years did my *Yankees* fail to make it to the World Series. And for half of those years, my brother's Brooklyn *Dodgers* were their opponents. It was weird how those baseball games between the far-away city of New York and one of its suburbs were called a "world series," but it was even crazier how we'd stream out of our classrooms between periods and congregate around whichever rich kid had a radio, mesmerized by the announcer's crackling voice.

And check it out — in all those years my brother's *Dodgers* only managed to win the series once—another sport in which Johnny kept losing to his brother!

I remember, at the age of fifteen, listening to the biggest game in the history of baseball. In 1956 the *Yankees* were, as usual, playing the *Dodgers* and in the sixth game, with Vince Skully announcing the play-by-play, *Yankee* pitcher Don Larsen was retiring every batter he faced. The excitement was palpable in Skully's voice as the *Dodgers* came to bat in the ninth inning. I was so nervous I could barely listen. Finally, Larsen struck out the last batter to become the only player ever to pitch a no-hit, no-run World Series game. And from then on, whenever I threw a baseball in a backyard game of catch, I pretended I was Don Larsen in the bottom of the ninth, mixing up my pitches and throwing the final out for a perfect no-hit, no-run World Series game.

Another milestone event that I'll never forget was the Miracle Mile. I was thirteen when Vancouver hosted the British Empire Games in August 1954. In May of that year I read in the newspaper that England's Roger Bannister had become the first human in history to run a mile in under four minutes. I knew how long a mile was. It was the distance from my home to the Fraser River, which I could see in the distance by looking down Macdonald Street. Unbelievable, I thought, that a person could run that far in only four minutes, when it took us kids about an hour to cover the same distance, walking home from the river with our slingshots or bows and arrows.

Incredibly, only a month later, John Landy of Australia lowered the new record to 3 minutes and 58 seconds! The stage was set for the running of the Miracle Mile in August at the Empire Games. I was caught up in all the hype.

On the big day, my dad and mum, Johnny and I were jammed into Empire Stadium with 35,000 other spectators for the track and field finals. The largest crowd ever to watch a sporting event in Canada was buzzing with excitement, eagerly anticipating the mid-afternoon show-down between the two fastest men in the world. It was the first sports event ever to be televised live across Canada.

Much has been written about the race that day; about Landy at the top of the back stretch peeking back over his inside shoulder just as Bannister surged by on the other side with his patented kick. But on that day it wasn't about who won. It was about how fast, and what I remember most was the pregnant silence when the loud-speaker announced the winner.

". . . in a time of three minutes and . . ." No one heard the rest. The crowd rose in an explosive cheer. We had just witnessed the impossible four-minute mile!

And when the celebration died down, the p.a. announcer tried again, "The time of the second-place finisher was three . . ." Now the crowd really went wild. Throughout the entire history of this planet, no human had ever run a mile in under four minutes — until a couple of months ago — and now two of them in the same race, right in front of our eyes![20]

A huge facet of my sporting life has always been my passion for the rules of the game. I am obsessed with the nuances of the regulations of even the most obscure contests, and there are very few sports where I don't think I know more than the referees themselves. I don't know what caused my need to know everything about the rules, but I do know what a pain in the ass I have been to my team mates, insisting that they always do it my way. And it hasn't exactly endeared me to opposing players either.

---

[20] Over the years the record time for the mile has continued to plummet, until it reached 3 minutes 43 seconds in 1999. The mile is no longer a standard length for competition.

My obsession with rules probably started at an early age with the endless bickering between brothers over who jumped the highest or threw the farthest, or who-killed-who in cowboys and Indians. I became expert at making up rules as the game progressed, which was important in school-yard ball games, where "I tagged you! . . . No yuh dinnint! . . . Yes I did!" was not a satisfactory way of resolving disputes. Instead, I discovered that, properly used, a fast mouth could outscore fast feet.

When I was thirteen I got an unforgettable early lesson in rules. It was in 1954, the year that the Canadian Open Golf Tournament was held at the Point Grey Golf Club in Vancouver — the last time our national open was won by a Canadian.[21] I signed up to be a caddy and, with about fifty other kids, attended two days of instructions on golf etiquette and caddying. I took the training very seriously, but I failed to make the cut because I was too small. So instead they paid me to print the scores, hole by hole, on the big leader board in front of the club-house. At thirteen years old, I was trusted to take the cards from the best golfers in the country, check their arithmetic and write their scores in big numbers for the whole world to see. I had become an RCGA[22] golf official.

Despite my caddying experience and despite my infallible knowl-edge of the rules, ten years later I would make one of the most unforgivable blunders in golf. I caddied in The Tasmanian Public Schools Old Boys Golf Tournament, and while I was tending the pin for a long putt on the 16th hole, the ball hit the pin and dropped in the cup. The resulting two stroke penalty, caused by me but assessed against the player who stroked the putt, cost him the low gross championship by one stroke! I'll never forget the look on his face: a mixture of disappointment and utter disgust at my incompetence.

Sailing was another sport where I picked up an early fascination with rules. One of my school friends, "Junior" Campbell, who spent a couple of weeks as my guest each summer at Pasley Island, was a

[21] Pat Fletcher, from Saskatoon.
[22] Royal Canadian Golf Association.

108

sailing prodigy and taught us the finer points of improving a boat's performance. Junior's dad was a veteran sailor who owned a 33-foot two-masted yawl named *Blue Wave* and, in my childhood summers, I joined their family for a week's sailing among the Gulf Islands. Those trips always started and ended with races across the Gulf of Georgia, pitted against a dozen other boats. The Campbells taught me just about everything that a kid could learn about the set of the sails and the principles of sailing, about the differences in rigging and about rights-of-way and the rules of racing.

I soaked up the rules like a sponge. In later years, whenever I was on the water, I'm sure that my incessant insights into our vessel's right-of-way relative to the shipping around us have been an absolute bore to anyone within earshot.

Given my fixation on rules, it was inevitable that I would some day become a referee. When my daughters took up soccer, I completed a week-long course for soccer referees at Shawnigan Lake School. I wanted so badly to be the world's best referee that, before one particularly important match, I practiced by refereeing a phantom game in the dark of night in the park across the street from our house. I ran up and down the field in my referee's uniform, blowing my whistle for imaginary off-sides and fouls, handing out yellow cards for unsportsmanlike conduct, even playing out hypothetical corner kicks and a make-believe penalty shot. After 45 minutes, I blew the whistle and changed ends for the second half of pitch black fantasy. My kids thought I was crazy.

Sports defined my childhood. Every morning in the school yard, before the bell rang, I was embroiled with classmates in life-or-death games of touch football or scrub baseball. Every recess and lunch hour found me on the baseball diamond playing flies-are-up, or three-and-you're-in on the soccer field. After school, it was rugby or cricket or cross-country runs. And at home in the evenings and on weekends we did it all over again, hour after hour, shooting hoops, playing catch, tossing footballs, and grinding each other down in merciless contests of slaughter-ball — stopping only when our mothers' whistles summoned us for meals, and continuing until after the street lights came on.

But I was never a star.

I was just an enthusiastic, energetic kid with a modicum of hand-eye coordination and a huge desire to play. I was such a skinny little geek that my classmates called me "Runt." The relentless throwing and catching of balls took an early toll on my puny body. Some limb or digit always seemed to be sprained or swollen and, in my final two years of school, my right elbow made a creaking noise like a rusty gate and became so painful that I could no longer throw a ball. It prevented me from playing on the school cricket team and forced me to quit the cadet corps because I couldn't bend my arm to salute. My dad would often say that unless I slowed down, by the time I reached forty I wouldn't be able to walk or dress myself. As it turned out, he was only out by a few years.

I have been very lucky. I loved sports because if I played hard, I did well, and that felt good. And when I did well, I got recognition, and that felt even better.

My success in sports as a child gave me the confidence to overcome my lack of stature and my shyness, and to become more assertive with people. For me, sports were a doorway to new friends and acquaintances. Like the year after I completed university, when I found myself working on a sheep station in the outback of Tasmania. You're not likely to meet many people deep in the hills in sheep country but, in my six weeks in Tasmania, I made scores of friends by playing baseball and Aussie Rules for the University in Hobart, rugby for the Army, and golf in the tournament previously mentioned.

Even in my 50th year, the jack-of-all-sports-and-master-of-none was still making friends through sport. During a two-week stay at Club Med Ixtapa my journal records that I played tennis, basketball, soccer, baseball, football, beach volleyball, softball and water polo; and that I sailed hobie cats, won the windsurfing race and learned the knee-hang catch on the flying trapeze. That's a pretty wide doorway for making new friends.

And finally, sports have always provided a sanctuary, a place where I could go to relieve the pressures of daily living. I have been very

OSAC Shirts and Skins — 1983
Soccer/Basketball every Thursday evening since 1967!

fortunate for the past forty years to have had a regular sports night out every Thursday evening with the boys of the Osler Street Athletic Club. Shirts vs Skins — basketball in winter and soccer in summer.

The Osler Street Athletic Club is a group of jocks, most of whom I knew in my university days. When we graduated, some of my Engineering classmates rented an apartment in a Shaughnessy mansion on Osler Street, where the coach house in the back yard was occupied by a couple of dental school graduates. A football challenge was issued and a rivalry developed, which has expanded to other activities and endured ever since.

For almost half a century, as each week progressed and the familiar stresses began to build — the burden of office responsibilities and the chaos of children and chores — it was always soothing to know that Thursday would soon arrive, and tensions would dissolve in an evening of physical activity, mental therapy and male bonding.

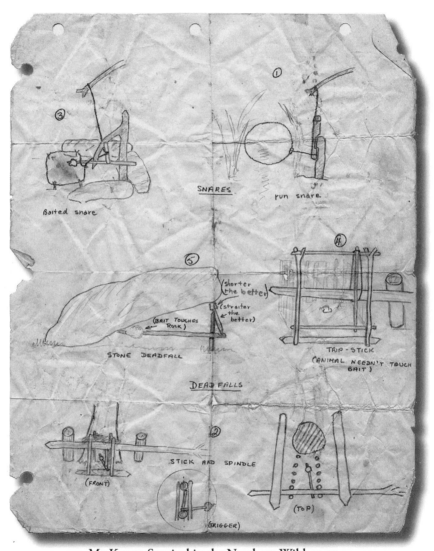

My Key to Survival in the Northern Wilderness

My original sketch of the deadfalls and piano-wire snares that we used to trap muskrats and other small animals (Drawn in 1956)

Chapter 12

Survival British Columbia

In June 1969, many years after I graduated from childhood, I was hiking with friends in the mountains west of Lilloett. We camped in a meadow beside Spruce Lake. The meadow was full of wild rabbits, and I boasted that I'd catch a rabbit for supper. At the edge of the meadow I set a snare with a wire noose and a supple branch to spring the bunny into the air and break its neck.

The next evening we crowded around our camp-fire and supped on roast rabbit.

As a kid growing up during the Cold War, I worried that the Russians would attack North America and that I'd have to escape to the wilderness. In order to survive alone in the northern woods, I'd need to live off the land. So I learned how to snare small animals and birds. It was one of many skills that I picked up from Mark Trail's weekly feature in the Vancouver *Province*.

Like most kids, we played with home-made bows and arrows. Our bows were made of willow branches and the arrows were split from cedar shingles. When I was thirteen we found a yew tree in the University Woods and from its seasoned branches we carved long bows, like those used by medieval English archers like Robin Hood and his Merry Men. We made lethal arrows with steel heads and feathered shafts. That summer I read about William Tell, a fourteenth century Swiss hero who was forced to shoot an arrow through an apple placed on his son's head. Of course we were soon practicing our marksmanship by shooting holes through most of the low-hanging apples in Mrs Turvey's orchard.

When I was thirteen or fourteen, the neighbourhood gang began to drift apart. My best friend, Donald, and I found ourselves spending more time together on our own, hunting in earnest with bow and arrow. In the autumn we could hear the popping of shotguns from the Fraser River, as ducks and geese faced the daily hail of lead from hunters in the marshes around the McCleery farm. We joined the fray, sneaking through the long grass and hiding in the ditches, firing arrows at the evening flights of ducks as they flew into the fields to feed.

It was always a long shot for a kid with a home made bow and arrows to bring down a duck in flight. I remember one time that I sent an arrow into a flock of widgeon high above us. Just as my arrow reached the top of its trajectory and turned in the grip of gravity for its return to earth, a duck bumped into it. Uninjured, but no doubt surprised by the encounter, the poor duck plummeted a few feet before flying on, apparently unscathed.

Donald was a better shot. We still reminisce about the robin he felled with an arrow while hunting on the McCleery farm. It was a frosty day — difficult conditions for fingers releasing an arrow from a taut bow-string. One moment the robin sat on the lower branch of a mountain ash tree — the next it toppled to the ground, its head skewered on Donald's arrow! Incredible shot.

William Tell's worst nightmare.

Donald's memory is that we gathered some dry branches, lit a camp fire and cooked the dead robin. He remembers that its meat was dark and stringy and had a gamey taste. That's not my recollection but, nonetheless, he still insists that we ate the bird. Maybe we did — God knows, we cooked and ate enough wild things that his memory could well be right.

When I was eight years old I joined a cub pack where I learned about knots and camp-craft. I took cubs and scouts very seriously. I practiced tying the most important knots until I could do them in my sleep — like the reef, clove hitch, bowline, sheet bend and sheep shank. I loved the images conjured up by the names of knots, images of adventure and exploration, of square-rigged sailing ships and galloping highwaymen! To this day I use these knots in so many activities, from boating to camping to tying horses at hitching rails. In order to earn my scout's badge for knots I also became skilled in splicing ropes and whipping their ends to prevent them from unravelling.

During my first year in cubs, China invaded Korea. The Canadian Army went off to war again, barely four years since my dad had come home from fighting the Germans. I was afraid of another war, so I gleaned from cubs and scouts everything I could to be prepared.

I learned semaphore. I'm sure I was the only cub in my pack who took semaphore seriously, but that year I saw a convincing demonstration of its value. We were sailing to Pasley Island in a small coastal freighter with several other families. Our vessel ran up on a rock and started to sink. We had to abandon ship. The lifeboat first took women and children to a nearby beach, and as it returned to the freighter for the rest of the survivors, I noticed one of the men who remained with us, Major Bell-Irving, using his arms to send a signal to the departing lifeboat.

Right arm horizontal — left arm diagonally upwards — left arm diagonal again — then both arms straight out to the sides. The distant boat crew waved acknowledgement. Wow, I thought, he's actually using semaphore. This stuff we're learning in cubs is really useful!

"Why did you signal B-E-E-R?" I asked Major Bell-Irving.

"If we're going to spend a few hours marooned, we might as well have some grog!" he replied.

Another useful skill that scouting taught me was how to build shelters. We learned to make bivouacs in the University Woods. Today these woods comprise the Pacific Spirit Park, and cutting trees or lighting fires is prohibited. But not so in the days of my childhood.

I remember one overnight campout in a frosty February in 1953, when eight of us scouts hiked a couple of hours through the University Woods from St George's School to the top of the cliffs above Spanish Banks. We set up camp in the forest near a slow trickle of water which gurgled from the frozen hillside. We hacked away at the trees with axes and hatchets until we had enough cedar boughs to build four or five lean-tos. The poles which supported each lean-to were lashed together with a dozen ropes — the more reef knots and clove hitches the better our chances of earning camp-craft badges. And with the lack of sensitivity to the environment that was typical of the times, we ravaged the trees for more boughs to keep our sleeping bags off the frozen ground. Then we logged the forest for firewood.

We became adept at building campfires. Some weekends the kids in our neighbourhood cooked lunch outdoors, in little groups beneath lean-tos made of fir-boughs in the O'Malley's vacant lot, or around the rotting stump in the Old Hag's Woods, or in the Turveys' orchard or on the banks of the Fraser River. Little camp-fires surrounded by keen little cooks wiping smoke from watering eyes while blowing at clusters of glowing coals and coaxing fire from reluctant twigs and branches. Billy-cans of boiling water or soup balanced on burning logs. Ash-covered wieners or twists of bannock falling into the fire as the forked sticks supporting them fell victim to the flames.

And on cool autumn evenings we'd congregate around the leaf fires that smouldered in most yards, prodding and poking with sticks, making little ovens for Mrs Turvey's apples or Mr Wollaston's potatoes.

By the time we were thirteen or fourteen, our wood-lore skills were increasingly directed toward wilderness survival. The Cold War was heating up, and fearing that the Russians could attack any day, I knew that soon I'd have to escape to the wilderness and live off the land. I'd read the story of the survival of the Swiss Family Robinson after their shipwreck on a lonely island, and earlier that year I'd seen the movie, *Robinson Crusoe*. Their survival experiences became my fantasy. If they could do it, so could I.

I learned to make fire without matches. In the rain-soaked part of the world where we live, lighting a fire without a flame source is extremely difficult. But Donald and I conducted serious experiments on rubbing two sticks together. Any schoolboy could saw the edge of his ruler back and forth across his desk to produce a burning smell and a wisp of smoke — but this never succeeded in burning down the school.

One afternoon Donald and I set out to create flames by following the instructions of Mark Trail. We pulled a drawstring back and forth across a rotating spindle, creating friction at the point where it drilled down into a specially carved groove in a cedar shingle. After two hours of relentless huffing and puffing, we actually turned the friction into a roaring fire.

It was like we were freeing ourselves from the bonds of civilization.

Finally we learned the ultimate wood-lore skill, the last essential requirement for survival when the Russians attack. Donald and I learned from Mark Trail how to set snares and deadfalls to kill wild birds and animals. Mark Trail taught us how to attach a noose of piano wire to a springy branch, and carve a hair-trigger from a twig. When an unsuspecting animal springs the snare, its neck is broken as it is swept off its feet. At the age of fifteen, Donald and I spent a couple of months snaring muskrats in the mud flats at the mouth of the Fraser River. The story of our trap-line is told in a later chapter.

We built deadfalls in the fields along the river bank, hoping to catch raccoons and pheasants. Our deadfalls were heavy logs propped on a trigger of whittled sticks and baited with carrots or grain. While our snares were surprisingly successful, the only animal we managed to bag in one of our deadfalls was a rogue tomcat, which I captured unhurt in our backyard.

At last I felt secure about my ability to escape from the Soviet invaders into the northern wilderness. I had learned to blend into the forest, to move silently and unseen by my enemy. I could find directions without a compass and light fires without matches. I could build a shelter and catch fish and hunt with bow and arrow. I could snare birds and animals for food and clothing. I felt good about my chances for survival when the bombs began to fall.

Sherpa Tensing — First Man on the Top of the World
*My sense of adventure lost its mystique when TV brought the world's
unexplored frontiers into my living room*

Chapter 13

Television Comes to Macdonald Street

When I was a kid, no one had TV. How could we possibly have imagined the extent to which TV would eventually change our world.

The world was a much different place during my childhood. It was a world of greater diversity and more exotic cultures — cultures that weren't yet diluted by the age of information and technology.

There were places on the planet where remote tribes still practised cannibalism or slave-trading or head-hunting. There were jungles untouched by civilization, where stone-age tribesmen in loin cloths still ate animals killed by poison blow-darts. There were deserts accessible only by camel caravans, whose treks to exotic markets were not yet impeded by pipelines or political borders. And there were mystical countries whose secrets had been revealed to only a handful of westerners.

We had no television to help us peer into the dark forests or scan the wide-open spaces to unravel the richness of those mysterious cultures. It was impossible to imagine that some day CNN would bring up-to-the-minute, on-location reporting of wars-in-progress in these unheard-of countries. Tourists could not travel to those far-off places because the globe was not yet girdled with freeways or circled with airlines.

Without television in their homes and villages, other cultures didn't get to see our way of life. So they didn't learn to covet our comforts and didn't feel the need to copy us. And so the life styles in foreign countries hadn't yet converged with ours.

By the time I was a teenager I hadn't been to the movies more than a dozen times. My contact with the rest of the world was through books. Our living-room shelves were filled with books from my dad's childhood, books like *The Wonder Book of Empire*, *Around the World in Eighty Days* and Stanley's *In Darkest Africa*. (At the time, much of Africa really was dark; and to circle the globe in only 80 days was a concept difficult to comprehend). The titles alone fuelled my imagination about discovery and adventure in exotic lands. Books — not television or movies — helped shape my images of the world. I lingered over the written words, conjuring up my own mental pictures, not bound by the visions of a Hollywood film director. Reading allowed me to pause and reflect as the stories unfolded, to develop ideas in the theatre of my mind, to savour and revisit them.

As the stories opened up the world for me, I developed a lust to visit far-off lands. It was Kipling who inspired my future travels through India and Afghanistan, an experience made so much richer from having read his stirring poems about the fabled Northwest Frontier. I don't believe that TV could have evoked for me the sense of drama and history that Kipling brought to life. I had committed to memory his entire "Ballad of East and West":

> . . . *They have taken the Oath of Brother-in-Blood*
> *on fire and fresh-cut sod,*
> *On the hilt and the haft of the Khyber knife*
> *and the Wondrous Names of God . . .*

I recited that lengthy poem to myself a hundred times, and with each recital I visualized romantic images of skirmishes with lawless Afghan tribesmen.

Years later, in 1965, when I was trekking around the world, I arrived in Afghanistan after an exhausting overland journey, I found myself emotionally overwhelmed by the rifle-toting tribesmen and ancient forts of the Khyber Pass. They seemed so familiar to me. It was like I had known them all my life. It was like a homecoming for me.

Another author whose skill with the pen lured me to a far frontier was Robert Service. His gritty poems, several of which also found their way into my memory, were the catalyst for my own future dog-sledding adventure in the Yukon, in 1989:

> *Were you ever out in the Great Alone,*
> *when the moon was awful clear,*
> *And the icy mountains hemmed you in*
> *with a silence you most could hear?*

Can TV say it like that? Wow, the word pictures!

Many adventures in my adult life were motivated by the books of my childhood. Another was my trip to the Crimean Peninsula in Ukraine in 1997. As a child I'd been captivated by my dad's recitals, whenever he had a couple of whiskies under his belt, of Lord Tennyson's poem, "The Charge of the Light Brigade." When the Iron Curtain came down, I was one of the first foreigners to be permitted to travel to the Crimea. I located the unmarked battlefield — 150 years had elapsed and it was now full of vineyards. I arranged for a horse, and galloped up the Valley of Death, wrapped up in my own world of guns and smoke, as I re-enacted Lord Cardigan's famous charge of the Crimean War:

> *Cannon to right of them, cannon to left of them,*
> *Cannon in front of them volley'd and thunder'd;*
> *Storm'd at with shot and shell, boldly they rode and well,*
> *Into the jaws of Death, into the mouth of Hell*
> *Rode the six hundred.*

And if you can bear with me for one more example, it was a charming little story about a duck named "Ping," a book I read and reread many times in my childhood. Ping lived with his mother and his father and two sisters and three brothers and eleven aunts and seven uncles and forty-two cousins on a boat-with-two-eyes on the Yangtze River. One day Ping got separated from his family, and became lost amongst all the strange craft on the big waterway. He came upon a raft from which cormorants were catching fish for their master. The cormorants couldn't swallow the fish because they had metal rings around their necks. The exotic images that this story evoked for me of fishing boats and beggars' boats, house boats and raft boats on the yellow waters of the Yangtze River never left me. They were so powerful that fifty years later, in 1991, they lured me to that magical river in China to experience for myself the wonder of fishing with cormorants.

I was twelve years old when television came to Macdonald Street in April 1953. This new invention would shrink the world and speed up the unravelling of its secrets. But it was also an invention which would conspire to hijack my imagination.

Our first encounter with this new gadget was recorded in brother Johnny's diary on Tuesday, April 7, 1953:

> *Got a haircut. Saw penguins at Stanley Park Zoo for first time*
> *Saw Television for first time.*
> *Raided the tree fort down in the Old Hag's woods.*
> *Played Go Go Stop etc with neighbourhood.*

Did you notice it? The ho-hum comment about his first brush with the gadget that would eventually have such profound influence on our lives! Even a lousy haircut was more important! The advent of television has had more impact on humanity than landing a man on the moon, but at least one little boy hardly noticed its arrival.

That 1953 diary entry raises a couple of other interesting thoughts about the impact of television. Do you think the sighting of the penguins would have been recorded if he'd seen them for the first time on the TV screen, instead of in the flesh, so to speak, at the zoo? Think about it for a moment.

Or how about this? If our family had settled into the habit of watching daytime TV, would Johnny have been playing with the neighbourhood that day? Would he have had the initiative to launch an attack on the tree fort in the Old Hag's woods?

The quality of that first television was poor, interrupted frequently by snowstorms of static and sparkle. In the first few years that television was available in Vancouver, it was common for the black and white images to fade in and out, to wave diagonally across the screen, or to tumble and roll like cherries in a slot machine. With only rabbit ears or rooftop antenna to pull in the signal, reception was poor and was always dependent on favourable atmospheric conditions. Before the CBC brought Canadian TV to British Columbia in December 1953, all telecasts came from the United States, and they could only be picked up by homes on hillsides facing south.

That first glimpse of TV gave no hint of what was to come. For a while TV couldn't even compete with my little hand-held Viewmaster, with its crystal-clear stereoscopic photos in full colour. And TV in its infancy certainly had none of the glamour of the trendy 3-D movies that were showing in theatres in 1953. Earlier that same month, Johnny and I had worn polarized glasses of red and green cellophane to watch *Bwana Devil*, a 3-D movie starring Bob Hope, in which lions appeared to jump out of the screen into the laps of the audience. In one scene, the audience ducked as a spear was hurled toward us — and with a strong sense of déjà vu, I turned to see if its shaft was impaled in Johnny's head, as Donald's spear had done a couple of years before.

I've no idea what TV program we watched that April day in 1953, but we clearly weren't impressed. For years I had dreamt of someday exploring the world, and my heart would have broken if I'd known then that this new technology would standardize and homogenize the world of my dreams.

How could we know then that TV cameras would eventually penetrate the farthest corners of the world, from the tops of the highest mountains to the depths of the deepest seas, from the lives of the rich and famous to the slums of Asia. TV would break down the mystique, and turn the uncommon into the commonplace by bringing it to our living-rooms in daily doses. Places which heretofore had strange values and customs would loose the very uniqueness which made them unknown and scary and exciting.

Let me give an example. In 2003, on the fiftieth anniversary of the first ascent of Mt Everest, live images of climbers were beamed directly from the summit of the world's highest mountain into my living room. As I watched the event on television, it was impossible to sense the incredibly difficult conditions that the climbers had overcome — the intense cold and hurricane winds; the strength-sapping scarcity of oxygen; the lack of sleep and nourishment. The TV pictures weren't making me feel the overpowering size of the mountain and the mind-numbing effects of dealing with the constant risks of crevasses and avalanches and storms. Television's ten-second sound byte captured neither the exhaustion of the climbers nor the exhilaration of their triumph.

I remember the day in 1953 when I learned that Mt Everest had been climbed for the first time. I was at Pasley Island following the coronation of Queen Elizabeth II, which had taken place at Westminster Abbey the day before, on June 2. I was fishing for shiners over the side of the wharf when someone told us he'd been listening to the coronation on his radio. He said they'd announced that a British expedition had reached the summit of Mt Everest on May 29, but the news had been withheld for a couple of days, to be released to the world as part of the Queen's coronation celebration.

The news that Everest was finally conquered gave me a strange, uneasy feeling. I couldn't put my finger on it exactly — on the one hand I was aroused, excited by the glorious achievement, while on the other I felt saddened that frontiers were shrinking and opportunities for further glory were being lost.

My generation may have been the lucky ones, the last kids who had to rely on our imaginations. The last kids who had the luxury of discovering things for ourselves. Our time wasn't stolen by passive hours in front of the tube, time that could be spent building things or playing or learning how to get along with one another.

But like everyone else, I couldn't resist the temptation of television. When Ricky Weir's family became the first on Macdonald Street to own a TV set (in 1954), we'd sneak onto their woodshed roof in the twilight of a summer evening and watch the movement of the black and white images through their closed window. Serenaded by the evening chorus of chirping birds or frogs from the neighbours' fish ponds, we'd huddle together and watch tiny cowboys and Indians galloping across the Weir's living room screen. And when Ricky's mother finally pulled the curtains against the darkness, we'd solemnly stand to attention for a hushed singing of "God Save the Queen" — as was the custom in those days at the close of each evening in the movie theatres!

It wasn't until my second last year of high school, in 1956, that my family acquired our first TV. Our choice of channels was limited and, for my interests, so was the quality of programming. Most of my friends sat in front of the tube watching programs like *The Mickey Mouse Club* or *American Bandstand,* but I preferred to be outdoors in the natural world.

The Vancouver Sun

TAtlow 7141   VANCOUVER, WEDNESDAY, OCTOBER 30, 1957   ***29

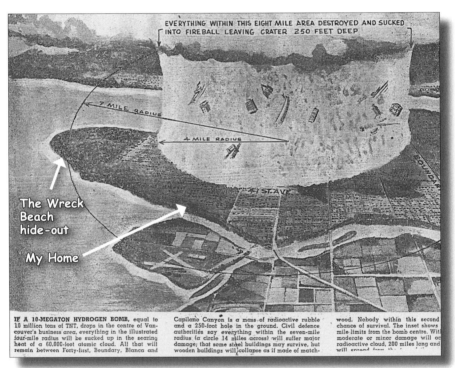

EVERYTHING WITHIN THIS EIGHT MILE AREA DESTROYED AND SUCKED INTO FIREBALL LEAVING CRATER 250 FEET DEEP

7 MILE RADIUS

4 MILE RADIUS

BOUNDARY

41ST AVE.

The Wreck Beach hide-out

My Home

IF A 10-MEGATON HYDROGEN BOMB, equal to 10 million tons of TNT, drops in the centre of Vancouver's business area, everything in the illustrated four-mile radius will be sucked up in the searing heat of a 60,000-foot atomic cloud. All that will remain between Forty-first, Boundary, Blanca and

Capilano Canyon is a mass of radioactive rubble and a 250-foot hole in the ground. Civil defence authorities say everything within the seven-mile radius (a circle 14 miles across) will suffer major damage; that some steel buildings may survive, but wooden buildings will collapse as if made of match-

wood. Nobody within this second chance of survival. The inset shows mile-limits from the bomb centre. With moderate or minor damage will oc radioactive cloud, 200 miles long and will spread from the…

Vancouver Meltdown
Articles like this in our daily newspapers during the Cold War
shaped my gloom for the future and encouraged me to hone my survival skills

Chapter 14

Beyond Hope

On September 18, 1953, the Vancouver *Province* carried a huge headline:

VANCOUVER, SEATTLE, LISTED
MAJOR ATOM BOMB TARGETS

It was yet one more distressing story in the continuing saga of doom and gloom for my hopes for the future. The headline article warned, "Vancouver is almost at the top of a list of Canadian cities considered most likely targets for the atomic bomb and the new hydrogen bombs that the Russians have just announced they are making."

As I entered my teens, I began to worry that Canada would be bombed, and perhaps invaded, by Russia. It was the beginning of the Cold War, and America and Russia were engaged in a feverish race to develop atomic and hydrogen warheads that would empower one side or the other to dominate the world. It was obvious that Canada would be caught in the crossfire.

Now, fifty years later, it seems hard to believe how strongly I was caught up in the rhetoric of the Cold War. To understand how war permeated my life, even though it would eventually turn out that no generation in history had such a safe existence as I did on the west coast of Canada, we must go back to the beginning.

My paranoia probably developed from a number of causes. Certainly the timing of my birth with respect to the Second World War was a factor. I knew that my father was away fighting the Germans and I knew why our mothers filled their time knitting socks and sending off parcels of food and warm clothing. I remember the ration coupons and shortages of things like food and fuel. I remember the blackout drills, when someone would knock on our door after dark, to inform my mother that too much light was escaping around the screens in the windows. And I have a vague memory of adults huddling around the big console radio in our living room each evening, listening to the latest bulletins from the battle front. I remember that when I misbehaved, I was told that the Huns eat babies who are naughty. It took me years to overcome my fear of the Huns.

Another influence on my awareness of war was my family's military background and the associated pride and paraphernalia. My mother's favourite brother had been killed fighting the same Germans in the other Great War. Our basement was full of his combat souvenirs, as well as those of my grandfather and an uncle on my father's side of the family — relics of the Boer War, the First World War and colonial India. They almost filled an entire room — steamer trunks and boxes of ancient flint-locks and muzzle-loading rifles, helmets and truncheons, pistols, swords, medals and big brass-artillery shells. Throughout my childhood, we incorporated all these artefacts of war into our games. And we often made basement fortresses from the cloth-bordered plywood blackout screens, which became a subtle reminder of the threat of attack from the air.

Our bookshelves were full of war stories, and I spent hours pouring over books about honour and courage and chivalry in battle. I loved reading *Glorious Battles of English History*, *Victoria Cross Winners* and *Thunder Boats Ho*, with photos of cavalry charges and battleships disintegrating in flames, and zeppelins fighting off WW I biplanes.

And paintings of famous battles hung on the walls in our home, keeping images of war fresh in our minds. Holding the place of honour at the head of our dining room table was a famous painting of the Battle of Waterloo. As I ate my supper every evening, I grew accustomed to that battle scene on the wall in front of me — guns and smoke, and men and horses dying in grotesque positions as a French cavalry unit attacks a square of kilted Scottish riflemen.

The impact of my father's war was so pervasive that, five years after it ended, it still strongly affected people's attitudes. I was caught up in the wave of patriotism and the general animosity against the Japanese. I clearly remember Donald's dad enlisting the neighbourhood kids to pull weeds from his front lawn. The Williams' garden was always well-manicured, but occasionally it was attacked by Japanese clover. It took a sharp eye to spot the tentacles of this tiny-leafed clover snaking through the grass, but Dr Williams encouraged us to "hunt down the little yellow Japs[23] and exterminate them before they multiplied." Whoever killed the most Japs got the biggest helping of ice cream.

When I was nine years old, Canada was back at war again. In 1950 the Korean War broke out and 25,000 Canadians were sent off to battle. By this age I was reading the headlines of the daily newspapers, which for the next three years were full of photos and stories of the fighting. I feared our family would be torn apart by another war. The Movietone News in the theatres, and the magazines that came to our home every week, had more images of fighting and war refugees. We got to add the Chinese to our list of stereotyped enemies. Popular comic books at the time, including *GI Joe* and *Joe Palooka*, dramatized heroic victories over the "little yellow geeks"[24] (and other, even more demeaning epithets).

About that time, the Russians disclosed that they had exploded their first atomic bomb. This news cast a big shadow over me. It gave

---

[23] While this term is unacceptable today, it was commonly used during and after the war with Japan.

[24] While this term is also unacceptable today, it was commonly used to describe the enemy during the Korean War.

me my first inkling that I was in serious danger. It was little more than five years since the atomic bombs had fallen on Japan, and all the war-time leaders continued to be in the news — Truman, Eisenhower, Stalin and Churchill were still around. My brother's birthday was August 9, the anniversary of the Nagasaki atom bomb, and year after year the newspapers celebrated Johnny's birthday with the same photographs of mushroom-shaped clouds. I asked myself continually what's to stop Stalin from dropping an A-bomb?

Images of American cities reduced to rubble by Russian bombers began to show up in magazines. Television hadn't yet come to Canada, but there were ads in the theatres showing cyclists and pedestrians dropping or running for cover with messages like "take shelter when you see a flash." At school we practised duck-and-cover drills, where we learned to hide under our desks, covering our heads with our arms. In August 1950 the *Vancouver Sun* carried an article about a Shaughnessy home-owner who built a bomb shelter in the lawn beside her home at 32nd and Marguerite Street. That was almost my own neighbourhood! All this hype was giving me nightmares about dying in a Russian bomb attack.

When I entered private school in Grade 5 in 1949, I became exposed to a new spin on the glory of war. Many of the teachers at St George's were war veterans. My housemaster, Captain Robinson for example, had a steel plate in his head and a glass eye from a First World War shrapnel wound. Nip Parker, the other housemaster, thumped around on a squeaky wooden leg, a memento of the Second World War.

Our private school teachers indoctrinated us with British imperialist traditions. We learned about classical warfare — the vastly outnumbered Greeks defeating Xerxes and his huge Persian army at Thermopylae — and battles that were fought to create and expand the British Empire. Our teachers preached the glory of war, and I loved to read stories about chivalry and honour and courage in battle. I even committed to memory one of my teachers' favourite poems, by Wilfred Owen, "Dulce et Decorum est Pro Patria Mori," which translates as "It is sweet and beautiful to die for one's country."

Every year on November 11, St George's School commemorated Remembrance Day with a very solemn and moving church service. It was attended by all the students, every one of us smartly dressed in the uniform of our cadet or boy scout unit. The school chaplain always read out the names of the twenty-seven boys and masters of St George's who had given their lives in the Second World War. David Else, who sat next to me in class every day, lost his father and two brothers in that war, and as their names were read out I always wondered just how *dulce et decorum* it must have felt for David and his mother.

I was torn between my private school culture of extolling the glories of war and my own nightmares about its terror and grief. And in a family that never displayed its emotions or talked about feelings, I wasn't able to share my fears with my parents. For my entire childhood, I suffered my dread of the Russian threat completely alone.

In the 1950s, my Uncle Charles was commander-in-chief of all British forces in the Far East. He was stationed in Singapore, where British and Ghurkha units were fighting communist guerrillas in Malaya.[25] Uncle Charles passed through Vancouver once or twice each year, on his way between Singapore and England. I always found his visits entertaining, sitting quietly while listening to him and Dad discussing world affairs. He brought first-hand knowledge of the communist threat in the Far East, and I'd listen apprehensively for clues about the likelihood of communism spreading to Canada. It was during one of those after-dinner discussions that I first heard the joke about optimists teaching their kids Russian while pessimists were teaching theirs Chinese. I wondered where I should go to start taking those Chinese lessons.

1953 was a frightening year for me. In January I read a headline in the *Vancouver Sun* that announced, "Courses Starting in Civil Defence." Apparently 3,000 volunteers were already enlisted, and they quickly wanted to train 10,000 citizens. It really looked like the Russians were coming! Why else would we need civil defence?

---

[25] At that time, Singapore was part of Malaya.

And then came the scary morning of June 2, 1953. I'll never forget being awakened at 4:30 that morning by air raid sirens. The wail of air-raid sirens is a frightening, chilling sound at any time — but in the pre-dawn darkness in your own home, alone in your bed, it's terrifying. The worst wake-up call ever.

It turned out, however, that this was the morning of Queen Elizabeth's coronation in Westminster Abbey, and at the moment when the crown was placed on her head, Vancouver's twenty-eight newly installed air-raid sirens went off in celebration. But it didn't take a genius to figure out that a more sinister use was intended for the sirens in future.

Sure enough, three weeks later, on the morning of June 20, in what they said was the biggest peacetime civil defence exercise in history, three minutes of continuously undulating sirens brought traffic to a standstill and cleared Vancouver's streets for fifteen minutes, simulating a major air-raid.

This was followed by the September headline which I quote at the beginning of this chapter: "VANCOUVER, SEATTLE, LISTED MAJOR ATOM BOMB TARGETS."

And then, in March 1954, there appeared a map in the *Vancouver Sun* which showed the radius of destruction if one of the new hydrogen bombs was dropped on Vancouver. Apparently an H-bomb test in the South Pacific had burned Japanese fishermen over eighty miles away, so the new danger zone had a 450 mile radius — from Prince Rupert to Calgary to Grant's Pass, Oregon! How scary was that for a thirteen-year-old?

Over the next few years, the newspapers were full of stories about mock A-bomb attacks and the casualties that would have resulted. A direct hit at Granville and Robson Streets on June 14, 1954, was predicted to have killed 62,450 people and injured thousands more. Another imaginary A-bomb hit Vancouver in November that year, and in June 1955 the papers reported mock attacks on many cities across North America. The bomb that hit Vancouver that month was assumed to have killed 17,400, maimed 11,900 and left 30,000 homeless.

Naturally, all this gloom and doom was pretty devastating for me. I never felt like making plans for the future because I wasn't sure that there'd be one. I often found myself day-dreaming of escape to the wilderness, where I expected to survive on the wood lore skills that Donald and I were developing. Towards the end of my school years these dreams would include my latest heart-throb — some beautiful, but as yet unattainable girl — who would run off to the wilderness with me and who would forever be indebted to me for saving her life.

In 1954, Canada *did* suffer a crushing defeat by the Russians. I was a hockey fan, and ever since I could remember, Canada had enjoyed the distinction of having the best hockey players in the world. That was one of the things that made me proud to be a Canadian. Canada enjoyed a long string of lopsided international hockey victories, but the first time the Russians showed up at the world competitions, in 1954, they beat us! Being beaten by the Russians their first time out was not only humiliating, it was foreboding. If they overcome us at the very thing that we excelled at, then what chance would we have to win at war?

The following year, in 1955, our Penticton *V*s played Russia in the final game of the world tournament. To win the championship we would have to beat the Russians by at least three goals. I'll never forget the excitement of listening to the broadcast of that game over CBC radio. Canada won 5 to 1. I remember the feeling of unbelievable patriotism and pride that day. Perhaps the Russians aren't so powerful after all.

But it would prove to be our last victory in anything over the Soviets for a long time. After a brief glimpse of sunshine, the dark cloud of fear and uncertainty soon returned.

Air raid sirens were being tested and evacuation routes planned. The Civil Defence movement was gaining momentum and training programs were being vigorously promoted. Even our postal stamps were franked with the slogan "You need Civil Defence — Civil Defence needs you." It seemed that CD pamphlets, displays and demonstrations were everywhere. In April 1956, The Vancouver

Province printed a big map of evacuation routes from Vancouver. It was estimated that 616,000 people could be evacuated in eight hours. Really? I calculated that if we got the one hours' warning that they promised, only one-eighth of them, or 75,000 would actually make it to safety!

In 1957 the newspapers continued the frenzy:

Russia Warns Danes of H-bomb Retaliation
Vancouver News Herald, April 1, 1957

Russia Warns West of its Atomic Might
Vancouver Sun, April 5, 1957

US has Power to Wipe Out Russia if West Under Attack
Vancouver Sun, May 3, 1957

We'll Use H-Bombs' NATO Tells Russia
Vancouver *Province*, May 4, 1957

It wasn't until forty or fifty years later that I discovered I wasn't suffering alone. Apparently, many of my childhood friends were quietly having the same fears about the Russians attacking, but it wouldn't have been cool to admit it.

In 1957, we learned that Russia had won the race to be the first nation to successfully test an intercontinental ballistic missile (ICBM) capable of delivering nuclear warheads. Nuclear bombs no longer required long-range bombers.

Suddenly Canada was vulnerable to air attack from almost any part of the globe — our oceans and northern wilderness were no longer natural defensive protection. A new debate began: "Was evacuation of our cities possible in the face of ICBMs?" It now appeared that escape was impossible — we couldn't hide in shelters and we couldn't run. In the years since my childhood we have learned to live with this dilemma, but back in the 1950s it was a new and scary concept.

October 4, 1957, was designated "National Civil Defence Day" in Canada. Brochures were delivered to all households confirming that, despite the obsolescence of bombers in the face of the new ICBMs, evacuation of all big cities was still the plan. They were sticking with the pitch that the Distant Early Warning Line (DEW Line) would give us all one hour's warning.

Vancouver was the hardest city in Canada to evacuate, because three of its four sides were bordered by mountains, an ocean and a river. On the fourth side there were no freeways and the bridges were bottlenecks. A map showing Vancouver's evacuation routes had been published in the newspapers the previous week. It was obvious to me that the plan wouldn't work. I could visualize the streams of cars converging at the east end of the Fraser Valley, funnelling into the two narrow roads that snaked east and northward into the mountains beyond Hope.[26]

Beyond Hope, indeed! I thought it ludicrous to think that the whole lower mainland could escape the bombs by crowding those roads. If traffic didn't grind to a halt through sheer volume, what about overheated engines, empty fuel tanks and minor accidents blocking the way?

And wouldn't the refugees be in the direct path of the prevailing west winds carrying radiation from the mushroom-shaped clouds? I thought back to the grainy black and white films we had watched at school, showing streams of refugees crowding the roads of Europe, being strafed and bombed by German Stuka dive-bombers. I couldn't bear to be part of that.

On October 5, in this our final year of high school, Donald and I therefore started to build a canoe. With a canoe, we could escape in the other direction, away from the clogged roads, away from the refugees and the radiation. We'd go west, up the coast where survival would be easy in remote inlets, eating fish and clams and oysters. My whole childhood had prepared me for that — rubbing sticks together

---

[26] Hope is a town at the east end of the Fraser valley, 160 km east of Vancouver.

to make fire, making sling-shots and hunting with bows and arrows, snaring muskrats and rabbits. I may have been insecure about a Soviet invasion, but one thing that I was very certain about was my ability to survive by living off the land.

One other event occurred on October 4, 1957, the day before Donald and I started to build our canoe. That was the day that Russia launched *Sputnik*, the first satellite to orbit the Earth. It was the day that Russia proved beyond all doubt that they were the most powerful nation in the world. And one month later, on November 3, 1957, they showed it was no fluke by launching *Sputnik II*, a craft that weighed over half a ton and carried a live dog named Laika. America, on the other hand, didn't launch its first satellite, *Explorer I*, weighing a measly eight pounds, until January 1958.

Too little, too late.

Shortly before we completed construction of our canoe, an article appeared in the *Vancouver Sun* on October 30, 1957. It was titled, "What to Do if That Bomb Ever Lands." It warned how important it was to follow the evacuation plans that were recently sent to house-holders. To read it now, fifty years later, it seems unbelievably naïve. It said that people would have "1½ hours of 'free time' after the warning sounds, for families to become united," before hopping in their cars and scooting out of town. It said traffic would have to keep moving at 25 miles-per-hour over the bridges, and it acknowledged that it would take 43 hours to clear the traffic bottleneck on the Hope-Princeton Highway!

No way was I going to be part of that!

Accompanying the article was a simulated aerial photograph of the city, showing the extent of devastation caused by a 10 megaton hydrogen bomb. Our home on Macdonald Street was within the seven-mile radius where "Civil Defence Authorities say everything will suffer major damage . . . wooden buildings will collapse as if made of matchwood . . . nobody has a chance of survival."

But with an hour's warning, Donald and I might be able to launch our canoe in the Fraser River at the foot of Macdonald Street. We'd head west, downriver, and if the tide was right we could be clear of that deadly seven-mile radius before the missiles arrive. We'd paddle upwind, and from the safety of the ocean we'd watch the mushroom-shaped cloud drift over the gridlocked streams of deserting traffic plugged at the choke points out of the city.

During the upcoming Easter holidays, Donald and I planned to head off into the wilderness for a week-long canoe trip. Two weeks before our departure there was a major air-raid siren test in Vancouver — the first since 1953. At 9 am on a Tuesday morning in March, a three-minute steady tone blasted across the city, warning that an air attack could occur within twelve hours. And then at 9:30 am came the most chilling of all sounds, the rising and falling wail of the "take cover" siren indicating that an attack was imminent.

That afternoon, the *Vancouver Sun*'s headline admitted:

Siren Test Shows:
CITY UNPREPARED
FOR AIR ATTACK

But two of us were prepared. With that amount of warning, Donald and I would have been certain to make a clean getaway to the west in our new canoe.

My New Raleigh
My first "real" bike broadened my horizons

Chapter 15

Day Trippin'

On my twelfth birthday my parents gave me my first bicycle. Well, my first that wasn't a rusty, used hand-me-down. It was an English Raleigh, metallic green with aluminum fenders. It was equipped with Sturmey-Archer three-speed gears, a chain guard, a kickstand and a shiny chrome bell. It was smooth and sleek and fast. No hill was too steep, no mud too deep, no trip too long for me and my Raleigh.

All the other kids rode CCMs. No one knew what CCM stood for. But my Raleigh was like a thoroughbred compared to their herd of plodding Clydesdales. Their CCMs didn't have hand brakes or gears. Or chain guards — they had to roll up their pant legs so their trousers wouldn't get caught in the chain.

Twelve years is a long time to wait for your first real bike, but it was worth the wait. Before that, I was forced to ride my brother's left-overs or plead with the other kids to let me borrow their bikes. But my twelfth birthday was the only time in my life that I ever got something top-of-the-line, something better than anyone else. I proudly wheeled my shiny Raleigh into the Carnarvon Street Fire Hall and paid fifty cents of my hard-earned pocket money for its first licence. Every time I rode that bike I felt special.

There was a time in my childhood when bikes were everything. In my neighbourhood we spent hours on our bikes playing follow-the-leader along the pathways, across the lawns and down the steps in the large gardens on Macdonald Street. We played endless games of bike-tag and bike-polo, using a tin can for the ball. We attached boxing gloves to the ends of poles and charged each other in medieval jousting bouts. We rode laps on the circular driveway around Elsie's house, day after day, pretending we were in the Tour de France, not knowing the Tour was a road race rather than an oval.

But by the time I was twelve years old, bikes weren't cool any more. But I'd waited too long to let that detail bother me. Very few teens — and no adults — cycled anywhere. Only nerds rode their bikes to high school. My daily commute to St George's School involved two buses and a mile of walking — three-quarters of an hour each way. But on my new Raleigh the 2½ mile ride took only ten minutes. I was already a nerd, so cycling to school was an easy choice.

The biggest thing about my new bike was that it extended the boundaries of my world. In those days, parents didn't drive their children to activities or entertainment. Urban kids had to make their own way to school, to church, to cubs and scouts, to sporting events, to the library and the movies. Now I had the freedom to come and go as I pleased, without the constraint of bus schedules or lengthy walks.

It was my best friend, Donald, who led us to the farthest corners of my newly expanded world. In the whole west side of Vancouver he was probably the only other high-school member of the spoke-and-sprocket set. Donald and his CCM were my constant cycling companions.

Together, we often explored the University Woods, where the trails were rough and virtually deserted. We spent many Saturdays at the frog ponds where Tin Can Creek meandered through the forest behind what is now Southlands School. The largest pool was called Polio Pond. In the spring we filled our jars with its tadpoles and, in the summer, with frogs. We poled back and forth across Polio Pond on log rafts which had been abandoned along the shore, jigging for fish in the dark waters.

We often rode down to the flats, the farmland along the Fraser River where, in 1862, the McCleery brothers had built the first European homestead in Vancouver. During our childhood, the old farm was still being operated as a dairy farm by a McCleery grandson, Gerry Logan. Donald's brother knew the Logans, and sometimes they enlisted our help with the haying or the milking. Or we'd cycle through the fields to the dike and sling arrows at ducks and pheasants. Or fill more jars with wiggly things like stickle-backs and salamanders from the sloughs and ditches. The half-mile ride home was always a killer — there was no way to avoid the steep hill below 49th Avenue. I hated climbing that hill. It took every ounce of my energy to reach the top, zig-zagging my light-weight Raleigh in its lowest gear, back and forth from one side of the pavement to the other, while Donald pumped with the strength of an ox on the pedals of his lumbering CCM, before finally conceding half way up.

Sometimes we rode to Mud Island — now Deering Island — at the foot of Blenheim Street, where we played capture-the-flag amongst the rabbit burrows on the broom-covered sand dunes. Japanese fishing families had lived on the island before Pearl Harbour, and the remains of their weather-beaten shacks were still there. Further west, at the foot of Crown Streeet was the old Musqueam Indian village, a cluttered assortment of unpainted sheds and shacks with no sewage and only sparse electricity. The Indian kids threatened to scalp us with jack-knives and scissors, but it was their packs of starving dogs that gave me the willies, snapping at our heels as we pedaled furiously to safety. Beyond the Indian village were the Chinese vegetable gardens which Donald and I sometimes raided in the autumn fogs. We'd light a camp-fire along the dike and cook our booty of potatoes and turnips and brussels sprouts.

When we disappeared for a day on our bikes, my parents would seldom ask what we were up to. For all Mum knew, we could have been out stealing hub-caps, which was about the worst trouble a kid could get into in those days. But of course my parents knew they didn't need to worry about hub-caps.

On many a weekend morning I'd be half asleep in my upstairs bedroom when I'd hear the familiar whistle of a strange bird. Outside, behind a bush in our front yard, Donald was calling me to action. Just like Huck Finn had done a century before — meowing like a cat or hooting like an owl below Tom Sawyer's window. I'd poke my head out and return the signal. Then we'd make the plan for the day's outing and I'd quickly dress, stuff some food into my pack, grab my knife and matches and be at the rendezvous within fifteen minutes.

One of our favourite destinations was the western tip of the Point Grey peninsula, about three miles from our home along Marine Drive. Donald and I established a permanent hide-out in the woods above Wreck Beach, under the roots of a huge maple tree. We provisioned our secret lair with necessities like drinking cups and a billy-can, tea and sugar, a fire-grate and matches. We hid an axe and a stash of firewood. We cycled there often, and on each visit we'd light a fire and cook a lunch of hot dogs or bannock twisted around a stick over the fire. Then we'd sneak around and spy on birds and wild animals in the marshes, and observe the movements of ships out where the Fraser emptied its brown silt into the clear water of the Gulf. And always, when we left, we'd stash our supplies out of sight, camouflage the fire and cover our tracks, so there'd be no evidence that we kept a camp there.

When a photo appeared in the *Vancouver Sun* in 1957, showing the area of destruction from a hydrogen bomb dropped on downtown Vancouver, I noted with relief that our Wreck Beach hideout was just outside the seven-mile circle within which "nobody has a chance of survival." When the bombs fall, our hideout with its little stash of provisions, shielded by the cliff above, might just save my life.

Not far along the beach were abandoned Second World War gun emplacements, built to defend Vancouver from enemy warships. It was only a dozen years since a Japanese submarine had shelled Estevan Point on Vancouver Island, and from our maple tree on the bluff, I quietly continued the vigil.

We often ditched our bikes in the woods and jumped on the log booms which were moored in the mouth of the river. We could travel considerable distances across the booms, leaping from log to log, all the way out to the fast water of the North Arm. Boom-running required good coordination and balance, for some logs were more slippery than others, or less buoyant and sank under your weight. You'd never want to fall through the logs, for they could close in above you and you'd never see the light of day again. Donald's friend, John Gibson, drowned on the booms near Marpole when he was 14 or 15 years old. In the winter, hunters shot ducks over the booms, and we'd sometimes get sprayed with falling bird-shot or find ourselves wringing the necks of wounded birds to put them out of their misery. Returning at dusk from a couple of hours on the logs was a challenge because current and tides could open leads between the booms, requiring difficult choices between retreating or performing incredible leaps in the darkness.

In 1955, Donald bought a smelt net and, on summer evenings when the tide was rising, we'd ride our bikes to Spanish Banks to fish for smelt. The smelt spawn at the top of the beach as the tide turns, and for an hour or two we'd slip Donald's net between the cork lines of other fishermen, gnarly old men in hip waders from Mediterranean countries where a five-inch fish is a catch to be proud of. When the bobbing of the corks indicated that smelt were striking the net, we'd swim along the cork line to recover them. Then, soaking wet, we'd cycle home after dark with a haversack full of the tiny fish. I could never bring myself to eat those bony little smelts, but Mum and the Williams family loved their taste.

The Vancouver airport was another of our cycling destinations. It took an hour or so to ride from our home across the North Arm of the Fraser River to Sea Island via the old Marpole swing-span bridge at the foot of Hudson Street.[27] On one of these trips we encountered hundreds of rats feasting on the garbage in the river's flotsam along the dike. Donald owned a BB gun, so we returned a few days later to shoot rats. We disassembled the gun and inserted its barrel up

[27] The Marpole Bridge was long ago replaced by both the Oak Street and the Arthur Laing Bridges.

his pant-leg, while I concealed the wooden stock up mine. It was a difficult ride, stiff legged, along Marine Drive and over the old wooden bridge and across Sea Island to its south shore. We felt very conspicuous and were certain we'd be stopped by the police. And I'm sure the rats wished that we had been.

Speaking of bridges, I also cycled across the Lions Gate Bridge to West Vancouver in the days when it was a two-lane toll bridge, in the days when riding a bike that distance was considered ridiculous. In 1955 and '56 I supplemented my pocket money by caddying at local golf courses, mostly Point Grey and the old Shaughnessy course at Oak and 33rd Avenue. But it was rumoured that a caddy could make twice as much — up to three dollars a round — carrying clubs for the rich and famous at the exclusive Capilano Golf Course at the top of West Vancouver's British Properties.

So one Saturday I cycled over the Lions Gate Bridge and up the steep mountainside to make my fortune. At Capilano I caddied for a guy named Percy who was dressed in plus fours and looked like Bobby Jones. It turned out he was Percy Williams, the sprinter who'd won two gold medals for Canada in the 1928 Amsterdam Olympics. Percy may have been fast of foot, but unfortunately he didn't turn out to be so quick at opening his wallet for his caddy.

Donald augmented his weekly allowance by delivering newspapers in Grades 10 and 11. Six afternoons a week he'd pick up his papers at the *Vancouver Sun* paper-shack in the lane north of 41st Avenue off West Boulevard. I think he had 66 papers, which he delivered from the basket between his handle bars. When Donald was away on vacation, I delivered his papers for him. On Saturdays, the weekend comics made the papers so bulky that I had to carry half of them in a sack over my shoulder and push the other half on his bike. I figured this was the best use for Donald's CCM — it was a cart-horse for lugging newspapers. But it could have used my Raleigh's pedigree for handling the steep hills and long driveways at the South West Marine Drive mansions on his paper route.

When I was fifteen we cycled to China Creek, to experience the new velodrome which had been built for cycling competitions in the 1954 British Empire Games. On Monday evenings the velodrome was open to casual riders, and I'll never forget how scary it was to ride high on the turns at each end of the oval. The steeply banked turns must have had slopes of 45 degrees — steeper than the pitch of most roofs. And if you tangled with another rider or didn't keep your speed up, you could collect a skin-full of cedar slivers when you crashed and slid to the bottom.

No one wore helmets in those days — not for hockey, not for construction work, not for cycling. With the amount of cycling we did, we were lucky to have escaped from our childhood with nothing more serious than scrapes and bruises. My only accident with another vehicle occurred on the way to school one morning when I was in Grade 7. I was on my new Raleigh, turning left from Mackenzie onto 33rd Avenue, when suddenly there was a screech of tires and the next thing I knew I was lying on my back on the pavement.

A green Morris Minor had clipped me from behind. I stumbled to my feet as the driver and some bystanders came running. I didn't know whether or not I was hurt because I was too busy dealing with the embarrassment of all the attention. They told me to lie down, they wanted to check me over. I insisted I was OK. They wanted to check the damage to my bike. I was painfully self-conscious and flustered by their concern, and slithered out of their grasp and bumbled off, pushing my bike down the sidewalk.

The driver followed me for a bit, not convinced that I didn't need help. But I was so mortified by the scene we were making that I managed to give him the slip by pushing my bike through a front yard, past a house and into a back lane. It was only when I was alone in the alley that I realized my rear wheel was so badly buckled that it wouldn't rotate through the back forks. It turned out that I was not hurt, but my bike was; I had to push it to a repair shop for a new wheel. The thing that upset me most was that the accident made me late for school. That evening my dad said I should have got the car driver's phone number and let him pay for the repairs. I never thought of that.

Buntzen Lake
Donald fly fishing off our make-shift raft

Our longest day-trip was to Buntzen Lake, which we did in 1956 when I was in Grade 10. Donald was a keen fisherman and at that time Buntzen Lake, in the hills above the Imperial Oil refinery at IOCO, was a remote lake with plenty of fish and no road access. So one day during the Easter holidays we set off on our bikes to catch some fish.

After an exhausting three hour ride, the last of it up very steep hills in pouring rain, we hid our bikes in the woods and hiked through dense forest to the lake. It was an unspoilt pristine pond in a lonely wild valley.[28] We knew beforehand that, if Donald was going to be able to cast a fly, we'd have to get away from the heavily-forested shoreline.

---

[28] A paved road now provides car access to parking lots at the lake, which attracts hundreds of swimmers and sunbathers on sunny summer days.

So we'd brought hatchets and nails and twine to build ourselves a raft.

We hacked up a suitable log and attached an outrigger, similar to the driftwood rafts I'd made during my summers at Pasley. Then we lit a fire and cooked soup and hot dogs before shoving out into the lake. We let the southeast breeze push our raft, Donald casting royal coachmen and grey wulffs at elusive trout and me steering the clumsy craft. We were alone in the wilderness, with no sign that humans had been there before us. An hour or two later the wind deposited us at the north end of the lake, and we bushwhacked through the soaking underbrush back to our bikes. It was a long ride home with the rain beating in our faces. Darkness had fallen by the time we turned down Macdonald Street with almost 60 miles of cycling[29] and an unforgettable day behind us.

The following Easter, when we were in Grade 11, Donald and I embarked on our longest cycling trip, a five day excursion across Vancouver Island. We cycled downtown to the CPR docks at the foot of Burrard Street and boarded the new car ferry, the *Princess of Vancouver*, to Nanaimo. Then, with no particular destination in mind, we headed up-island carrying all our food and provisions in knapsacks on our backs.

We camped the first night near Nanoose Bay, in some woods beside the Esquimalt & Nanaimo rail line. In the middle of the night we were awakened by the blinding headlight and ground-shaking vibrations of an approaching train. The locomotive was almost upon us when its ear-shattering whistle pierced the darkness. Was it whistling at us? Were our sleeping bags too close to the track? Badly frightened, we jumped into the underbrush as the train thundered past. In the light of morning we realized the whistle had been for a nearby road crossing, but ever since, I've made a thorough reconnaissance of my surroundings before setting out my sleeping bag in the dark.

On the second day we cycled 30 miles up the road toward Alberni, past Coombs and Cameron Lake to Cathedral Grove, a majestic stand

---

[29] One mile equals 1.6 kilometres.

Breakfast in the Woods
We cooked a lot of meals over open fires

of first-growth cedars and 800-year-old Douglas firs that has since become famous as one of British Columbia's few accessible stands of virgin forest. Heavy clouds piled against the mountains as we set up camp beside a brook deep in Cathedral Grove. Rain began pelting down on the thick forest canopy above us. The lower branches of the big trees were festooned with dripping beards of rain-soaked Spanish moss which looked and sounded like an army of unshaven mountain-men slurping their soup.

We had no tent, so we built a shelter of cedar boughs to protect us from the rain. Crouching around our feeble fire of wet twigs which refused to burn, blinded by smoke which refused to rise through the dripping canopy above us, we gulped down half-raw spaghetti which refused to cook. Our clothes were soaked and the cheerless woods were so oppressive that we packed up before nightfall and retreated out of the gloomy forest.

The next three nights we huddled under a log on the beach beside Cameron Lake. We hollowed little nests in the gravel and slept under the cover of a small canvas groundsheet. And it rained and rained and rained. Mornings and evenings found us on our knees beneath our log, blowing at embers and fanning at flames. Donald fished for trout in the Little Qualicum River while I spent three cheerless days scanning the skies for a glimmer of sunshine. Then we'd retreat from the stormy weather and return to the smoke to rotate our boots and socks at the fire, juggling between drying them out and scorching their leather.

The rain seldom let up during those four days. With no way to escape the weather, I became obsessed with searching the skies, hoping to predict a break in the clouds and a glance at the sun. The experience fuelled my life-long fancy to forecast weather by studying the sky — the shape of the clouds, their height against the mountains, the impact of their direction and the shifts of the wind, and the meanings of the various shades of grey. As hard as I stared at the Cameron Lake clouds that week, I never found any silver lining.

Traveling home on the ferry from Nanaimo, we clapped each other on the back and declared what a fine trip it had been. How quickly a dry dining-room and a couple of hamburgers can make one forget!

This was my last cycling trip. I had just turned sixteen and would soon be borrowing the keys to the family car. I soon found that the '49 Plymouth handled soggy roads, steep hills and headwinds with a comfort and ease that caused my Raleigh's metallic green shine to quickly lose its lustre.

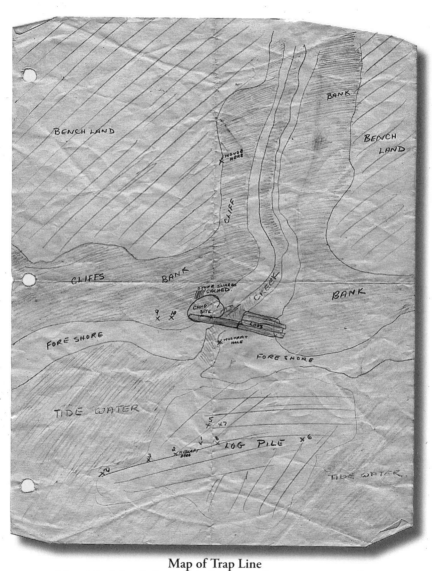

Map of Trap Line

*My original sketch showing the locations of snares on our trap line
near Wreck Beach at the mouth of the Fraser River*

Chapter 16

The Fur Trade

In his final two years at Magee High School, Donald's brother, Paul, ran a trap line on the flats by the Fraser River. Paul rode his bike down to the McCleery farm after school and on weekends to help with the milking and haying and, in return, he was allowed to set muskrat traps in the sloughs and ditches on the farm.

Paul's trap line comprised about a dozen traps, each set at the mouth of a muskrat den by the water's edge. They were leg-hold traps chained to stakes that were driven into the bank. Two or three times a week he'd rush home from school, pull on his high gum boots and bicycle down to check the traps. It was often long after dark that Paul trudged home up the steep Macdonald Street hill, soaked, soiled and smelly, a dead muskrat or two stuffed in his canvass haversack.

On some of these evenings, Donald and I would help with the skinning. Peeling off the pelts was a gruesome task. It was definitely not for the squeamish. I never became comfortable with the skinning process, but I'm going to share with you the grisly details because the memories are such a large part of my life.

The soggy limp bodies looked so pathetic. It was like someone should just bury them, get them out of sight. At first I was revolted at the thought of touching them — after all, they were rats. The thing that probably helped me through it was Paul's detached matter-of-fact way of cutting open dead creatures. The year before, I'd watched him perform an autopsy on his pet rabbit, and another time he gathered all the neighbourhood kids around him as he demonstrated how to skin a snake. We all discovered for the first time that snakes had ribs and backbones.

The mechanics of skinning muskrats were simple enough — we just made a slit with a sharp knife along the inside of each back leg, and then pulled. The hide peeled off like a glove being rolled from your hand. There were no guts to deal with, just a naked pink carcass that looked disturbingly like a new-born baby. One of the worst parts was the sickly-sweet smell that stuck to your fingers for days, and the bits of fat that greased your clothes after you worked the scraping knife over the hide.

I thought of Peter Rabbit in Mr McGregor's cabbage patch, and the pictures of the cuddly Flopsy Bunnies that he captured when they fell asleep "from the soporific effect of eating too many lettuces." He stuffed them into a gunny sack and was going to skin them, to line Mrs McGregor's coat. If kids knew what a skinned rabbit looks like, they wouldn't be reading *Peter Rabbit* at bed-time!

Stretched inside-out over boards made from orange crates, the pelts bore no resemblance to the happy little creatures that had frolicked in the McCleery farm's sloughs the day before. As soon as he had half a dozen skins, Paul would cycle down to the Hudson's Bay Company's raw-fur buyer at 321 Water Street. Ninety cents per hide was what they were worth, and sometimes the buyer gave him an extra dime for their size. Apparently the McCleery slough muskrats were larger than the prime winter pelts of their cousins from the frozen north. The proceeds from one muskrat skin could treat Donald and me to a Saturday afternoon matinee at the Kerrisdale Theatre, followed by glazed donuts and milkshakes next door at the Avenue Grill.

As Paul slung his hides across the counter, to be added to the huge bundles of beaver and martin and weasel and lynx stacked on the floor beyond, he was taking part in a transaction that had been repeated at fur-trading posts millions of times all across Canada. I knew from my Grade 8 history lessons that ever since the Hudson's Bay Company received its charter in 1670, it was the leg-hold trap, more than any other invention that had opened up Canada. I never enjoyed skinning a muskrat, but it was easier if I pretended that I was participating in the fur trade that was such an important part of Canada's history. I was doing my small part to add a stitch in the common thread that, over the centuries, had bound my frontier nation together. One year later, in 1957, the Hudson's Bay Company closed forever its Vancouver fur-trading post.

I started my own fur trade during the summer holidays of 1955. That summer I spent two weeks with a school chum, Roger McDonnell, at his grandparents' orchard on Okanagan Lake. Like all farmers, Roger's grandfather hated the gophers that burrowed beneath his fields and orchards, for they ate the roots of fruit trees and created holes where cattle could break their legs. His grandfather offered a fifty-cent bounty for every gopher that Roger and I could kill.

We didn't have a gun, so at first we tried our luck with slingshots. The gophers stood erect and still beside their burrows, but each time our shot was close there'd be a puff of dust as the gopher disappeared into its hole.

It was time to bring up the cavalry — a pair of rusty leg-hold traps hung in a dark corner of the barn. We set the iron jaws and staked the traps beside a couple of gopher holes, just as Paul did at the muskrat dens in the McCleery ditches. Almost immediately we had two captives. Two squirming, struggling wild-eyed critters with mangled bloody forelegs caught in the iron vice, tugging and straining at the chain that prevented them from retreating to the safety of their lair. I'll never forget those beady little eyes looking up at us with such terror and loathing, saying "Why are you doing this to me? What right do you have to put me through this torture?"

Paul had never told me about this part of the fur trade. Sure, like most boys, I'd killed the odd creature before. But this wasn't like snapping the necks of snakes or removing a carcass from a baited mouse trap. Never did I have to face my victims alive and suffering like this. But I had to go through with it now. I had to put the poor creatures out of their misery, quickly, with a garden hoe.

I felt so terribly sorry for what I'd done. I felt so much compassion for those two lifeless little bodies. We never set those gopher traps again.

But what about the pelts? Do gopher skins have value at the trading post? I taught Roger the intricacies of skinning, thinking we could somehow justify the killing. Those lives needn't be wasted — they could make a hat perhaps, maybe help someone survive in the cold. We stretched the pelts over boards and hung them to dry on his grandma's clothes line, like inside-out gloves, hanging between the bed sheets and the tea towels. But as they aged in the Okanagan heat, they soon began to smell. I tried to remember the instructions in *The Boys Own Annual* for curing the skins of small animals. Something about rubbing equal parts of alum and table salt into the fleshy side of the pelts. Roger and I didn't know what alum was, so we substituted pepper. But the smell continued to worsen, and when maggots emerged, we removed the furs to the cool of the root cellar, where they were soon forgotten. And for all I know, they may still be there today.

In the spring of the following year, 1956, in my Grade 10 science class, I was assigned a project to research wildlife in British Columbia. I wrote to the provincial Game Branch and received their latest statistics and annual reports and, by the time I had completed my assignment, I figured I was an expert on game and fisheries management. I still have my completed scrapbook, full of statistics such as bounties for vermin killed and numbers of fur pelts harvested. My report included sections on predators, big game, fish and game birds. But the major focus was on the fur trade. I pointed out that "muskrats are the backbone of the fur industry" producing 56,000 pelts in British Columbia in 1954. (Believe it or not, 351,000 squirrels were also killed for their fur that year.)

At the beginning of my report was a quote that I must have plagiarized from somewhere, but when I read it now, all full of sweetness and good, I wonder how I could have been so callous about trapping those poor little creatures:

> *To see a squirrel at play, to watch the vast bird migrations*
> *at the turn of the seasons, to view a hawk wheeling in the*
> *blue sky and hear the bird-sounds around you in the woods*
> *— these are things of the spirit and are of incalculable value,*
> *important to people in all walks of life.*

And as retribution for the agony I had inflicted on those Okanagan gophers, my report contained a prominent section on a new kind of humane trap. Invented by a fellow named Conibear, it was supposed to kill instantly, ending the cruelty of the fur-bearers' slow and agonizing death. Not yet patented, it was said to be "the greatest thing to hit the fur trade since the Hudson's Bay Company got its charter!"

In the fall of 1956, Donald and I experimented with our own style of humane traps. We decided to snare animals with nooses rather than torturing them with leg-hold traps. We found a promising location at the mouth of the Fraser River, near Wreck Beach.[30] It was a marshy area near the log booms, with an impressive number of animal tracks, mostly muskrat and raccoon. I kept a record of this new trapping venture, and my notes show that we set our first snares on October 27, and we made no less than sixteen visits to check them before December 2, when studying for school exams became a higher priority. As I look back on it, I can't imagine how we found the time for all those three-mile bike rides to check our trap lines, considering that my weeks were so full of rugby and homework and household chores.

The business of trapping animals was as gruesome as ever. All our traps were snares and deadfalls that we learned from "Wood Lore," the syndicated outdoors serial in the weekly coloured comic section of the Vancouver *Province* newspaper. The simplest snare was a run snare,

---

[30] See map of our trap line on page 150.

which was merely a piano-wire loop that tightened around an animal's neck as it walked or swam through the noose. For a more elaborate version that would break the animal's neck, a springy sapling could be added, which would flip the victim into the air when triggered. More sophisticated still was the baited spring snare, which would lure the victim to the carefully-set noose. The trickiest part was to set the trap in the right location so the animal would insert its head into the noose in the first place.

Our first sets were spring snares, intended for mink or weasel. We baited them with small fish that we caught in Tin Can Creek. We tried to trap raccoons in a deadfall against a fallen tree, using a bullhead for bait. And in a pile of logs below the tide line we set run snares for muskrats.

When we returned the next day we could hardly believe our luck! My memory is that we were wildly ecstatic at snaring our first muskrat, but the note that I made in my little journal that evening seems so callous when I read it now:

> *. . . the other run snare had a cold and dead muskrat tightly held around the neck. By surrounding signs it was decided this animal had been returning to his nest with food while the traps were conveniently submerged. He swam into the noose and as the tide rose he jumped above the water for air, thus tightening the noose and strangling himself . . .*

Sounds like a coroner's report!

I remember being absolutely elated that we'd caught something. We had set out to snare a muskrat and had actually succeeded. We'd found a run that led to its den, and we'd put the right-size noose in just the right place! And the poor animal was doomed — he couldn't wriggle free. Surely we now qualified as woodsmen!

But, as we removed the drowned muskrat and examined the circumstances of its death, I felt terrible. The claw marks on the slime-covered logs told of a desperate struggle. I prayed that the drowning was quick. But I had nightmares of the poor creature caught on an incoming tide, jumping frantically for gulps of air as the water slowly rose, constrained by the tightening noose around its neck. And what if it was a mother returning to her nest with food for her kits? Tiny stalks of fresh green eel grass lay in the mud beside the limp body.

I felt awful. Just like I'd felt with the gophers the previous summer. But somehow I couldn't stop. I thought to myself that not just any city-slicker can snare a wild animal. The thrill of the chase was stronger than the remorse over the outcome.

The crowning achievement of my trapping career occurred a week later, when I snared a mouse. Not glamorous perhaps, but certainly of the highest technical difficulty. We had found some small holes in a clay bank above the creek. They could have been anything — spider holes, swallow nests, who knows? But on a hunch, I set a spring snare over the entrance to one of them. The noose so fine and centered so precisely that the quarry won't pass it by, nor the wind or rain change its alignment. The trigger must be so delicate that the weight of a tiny mouse will set it off, but a falling leaf won't. The sapling which springs the victim off its feet must be strong enough to break the mouse's neck as it flips in the air, yet subtle enough not to bind on the trigger.

Imagine my surprise when, after three days absence we returned to the clay bank to find the lifeless body of a tiny mouse dangling from the end of the sprung sapling! Maybe not as exotic as trapping a wily wolverine or a valuable fisher, but infinitely more precise. And also, I thought, a nobler ending for the poor mouse than snapped up in a cheese-baited mousetrap or a slow death in a dish of strychnine behind the furnace.

My memories of trapping innocent creatures sadden me nowadays. But there is part of me that is proud that I was able to deal with my squeamishness and to succeed in an endeavour requiring such a unique skill. I also take some comfort in the words of Ernest Seton Thompson, ". . . no wild animal dies of old age — they all suffer a violent death."

Seaforth Cadets Ross and Ross
As students at St George's School, my brother Johnny and I
were obliged to join a cadets corps

Chapter 17

Help The King

Every student at St George's School was required to join the militia. So when I entered Grade 9, I too became a soldier. I followed in my brother's footsteps and joined the Seaforth Cadet Corps.

Cuidch'n Rich was the Seaforths' motto. Gaelic for "Help the King." Finally I could do something about my fears of a Russian attack. I could help the king beat off the invading army. But when I joined up, I don't think the king would have had any illusions about Cadet Ross inspiring terror in the hearts of the Soviets. For I was scarcely five feet three inches tall and weighed barely 95 pounds.[31]

But dressed in the uniform of my new highland regiment I was very proud. I loved marching to the skirl of the bagpipes, with the swirl of kilt and sporran[32] about my waist, the rhythm of marching feet and the thunder of a hundred boots snapping to attention.

I spent literally hours each week preparing my uniform, polishing leather and brass, cleaning and ironing and sewing on buttons. Buckles, buttons and crests had to be rubbed and polished, whiting applied to

---

[31] 160 cm tall & 43 km in weight.
[32] A leather pouch adorned with tassels and hair which hangs in front of a kilt.

belt and spats,[33] my sporran needing separate doses of Silvo and Brasso and black shoe polish — and a regular combing. And a few misplaced fingerprints would require that the whole thing be pulled apart and polished again.

Cadet night was Friday evening, and every week Johnny and I walked in our freshly pressed uniforms to 41st Avenue and caught the Macdonald Street bus to the Seaforth Armouries. Cadet parade always started with a formal inspection by the commanding officer, who was a colonel in the regular army. World War II had ended less than ten years before, and the army still appeared to be on full alert. Their attention to detail was fanatical. The slightest smudge on our brass or crease in our tunic could put the colonel into a rage. He even checked the soles of our shoes to ensure we hadn't forgotten to polish the insteps.

Following inspection there'd be an eternity of parade drill. We spent hours marching back and forth, wheeling and turning in columns and ranks, open order, close order — with rifles and without. We learned military posture at the end of a swagger stick — constantly being poked and prodded by foul-mouthed sergeant-majors who yelled obscenities and demeaned us with sexual epithets. The cadet corps contributed greatly to my knowledge of aberrant sexual behaviour, but it almost cost me my self-esteem.

I took the whole cadet thing so seriously. Nowadays, when I watch military units marching through town in seasonal parades like Gay Pride or Santa Clause pageants, I'm very critical of their formations. I'm quick to notice a marcher out of step, a ragged column or an un-pressed uniform. But in each marching unit there's always a skinny little geek with uniform perfectly pressed, shoes shone, brass sparkling, marching stiffly like a robot, precisely in step, chin in, chest out and eyes glued to the bum of the guy ahead.

That was me.

At our cadet meetings we also learned to clean and disassemble rifles, Bren guns and mortars. We were trucked on overnight trips to a

---

[33] Canvas gaiters covering instep and ankle.

firing range on the north shore, where we fired the Lee Enfield rifles that we marched with on parade. And back on Macdonald Street, Johnny and I and a couple of school friends would unpack Grandfather's rusty old breech-loading hammer-locks that were stashed in our basement dark room. We'd slope arms and present arms and march around our back yard, practising rifle drill for next Friday's inspection — and scare the hell out of the neighbours.

During my summer following Grade 10, I received six weeks of military training at the army camp in Vernon, BC.

For me, going off to cadet camp was like the photographs I'd seen of our fathers going off to war. We traveled by overnight train, a troop train with no civilians — eighteen carriages carrying a total of 400 cadets and army officers, all in regimental uniform. I was 15 years old and very nerdy and hadn't yet reached puberty. All the other cadets were older, bigger, hairier and tougher than me. They played poker and ran up and down the corridor from car to car, swearing and smoking and scaring the bejesus out of me.

When we arrived in Vernon the next morning, we were met by a convoy of army trucks, driven by 16-year-old cadets who were taking the Driver Mechanics course at the camp. Most of the cadet drivers looked tough and hairy, but the kid driving my 2½-ton truck could barely see over the steering wheel. We assembled on the parade ground at the army camp on Mission Hill and were assigned to our new units. I found myself in Number 8 Platoon, Charlie Company, quartered in one of the H-huts (Hut 34 I believe it was) close to the highway. I had a bottom bunk below Lawrence Pantherbone and next to Doug Schneider, with whom I became good buddies. Lawrence was a Cree Indian from the Blood Reserve near Cardston, Alberta, and Doug was from Rossland, BC.

At the camp there were 1,100 cadets (all male of course, for in those days it would have been unthinkable for women to enlist in the infantry) from BC, Alberta and the Yukon. For the first two weeks we were not allowed to leave the camp. Good thing, too, because I was terribly homesick. For the first few days I thought there was no way

161

Number 8 Platoon, Charlie Company, Vernon Cadet Camp — 1956
That's me (white circle), *thankful that I'm not wearing my kilt*

that I could last the seven weeks until the end of August, when the troop train would return us to Vancouver.

Reveille each morning was at 6 am. We'd hear the bugle call, but we'd stay in bed an extra minute or so until the sergeant-major tromped through the barrack yelling "Get your sorry asses out of bed, you little faggots!" or "Let go your cocks and grab your socks!" Then followed a half hour of sewing and mending and laundry before breakfast. We made our beds with hospital corners, top blankets stretched tightly enough to bounce a coin. Then everyone stood at attention at the foot of our beds for daily barrack inspection.

Then we'd assemble on the parade square for inspection of our dress and an hour of marching drill. I immersed myself in the spit and polish, the pressing and ironing, the courses and the weapons training and the endless marching and rifle drill on the parade ground and, before long, the first two weeks were up.

The Army paid each cadet $100 for attending the summer camp. It was an exciting occasion when the entire cadet corps assembled for Pay Parade at the end of our second week. Everyone was eager to leave the base and go downtown. We were all turned out in the full dress uniform of our respective regiments. Being one of the few cadets from highland regiments, I felt proud that the kilt and sporran and sparkling white spats of my Seaforth uniform drew attention to me.

One-by-one we marched up to the paymaster's table to be given the first $5 instalment on our summer's wages. Each cadet was given three paper dollars and two silver dollars (rumour had it that the Vernon Chamber of Commerce was tracking our expenditures). As we stood at ease, in our perfectly aligned rows, platoon by platoon, the training officers and NCOs strutted up and down, criticizing our deportment, abusing us and making lewd jokes about our virility and the local girls. World War II had ended only 10 years before, and our army camp NCOs were battle-hardened, regular-army veterans with serious attitude issues. Some were overbearing bullies, and one of them that day caused me the greatest embarrassment of my entire life.

A hulking sergeant-major with a beer-belly and a handle-bar moustache, who had considerable skill at making cadets the butt of his foul jokes, stopped in front of me and asked what I was wearing under my kilt. No Highlander wears underpants under his kilt, so I gave the expected reply, "Nothing, Sir!"

Except that I had a secret — amongst all those hundreds of big hairy 15- and 16-year-old cadets, I was probably the only one who hadn't yet reached puberty, and I hid my underdeveloped genitals by wearing undies. I couldn't imagine the ribbing and teasing that I would receive if they found out.

The sergeant-major then reached out and lifted the front of my kilt with the end of his swagger stick!

I thought I would die. My peers would see that I was hairless. My knees started to shake and I could feel my face and neck turn crimson.

"No highlander wears gotchies!" he yelled for all to hear. "A highland warrior lets his balls swing free!"

Swing free? Mine hadn't yet even descended. I had never felt so humiliated.

The sergeant-major ordered me to take a step forward. I was trembling like a leaf. He ordered me to remove my underpants! And then, to my utter horror, he raised my undies skyward on the tip of his swagger-stick, for everyone to see!

I don't know how I survived. I only remember the humiliation of having to carry my underpants in my hand for the remainder of the parade, like a white flag to identify me as the only soldier in camp with no hair on his crotch.

After a couple of weeks I had settled in to camp life. I enjoyed the courses in compass-reading, map-reading and semaphore. I learned how to strip down and assemble Lee Enfield rifles and Bren guns, again and again and again — blindfolded. I learned how to french my platoon-mates' beds, and joined in the fun of placing full wash basins — or better yet, bulging water-filled condoms (me hardly knowing their real purpose) — under the tightly-stretched blankets of carefully-made beds belonging to unsuspecting victims.

Army camp meant endless hours of marching on the dusty parade square in the relentless heat. Most mornings we assembled on Mission Hill for an hour or two of marching drill. In platoon and company strength we wheeled and turned and halted and presented arms and stood at attention and sloped arms, ad infinitum. It was very hot and absolutely shadeless and, although we were given salt tablets, the drinking of water was discouraged.

It was not uncommon for cadets to faint in the oppressive heat of the parade square, and I remember one Sunday church parade when Cadet Coyle, who was standing next to me, rolled his eyes and slowly twisted to the ground, unconscious. We were standing at attention, so no one could go to his assistance. In fact, I felt guilty merely allowing my eyes to stray in his direction. It was a weird feeling, stepping over him and his rifle as we were marched off to church. And I noticed that his wasn't the only prostrate body lying on the square.

At the rifle range I was a lousy shot, but I excelled when it was my turn to stand in the butts and raise and lower the targets by means of a chain. I was good at spotting the fresh bullet holes and indicating their locations with a long steel pointer to the distant shooter, several hundred yards away. One day in the butts a ricochet hit my leg, and I was disappointed that it didn't draw blood — a red badge of courage could have earned me a little prestige. I remember the daily lecture about the hazards of being careless with our rifles — and the story of the cadet, a couple of years before, who had turned suddenly and inadvertently shot his instructor dead, or the poor kid who was shot through his eye when he peeked over the top of the butts to see why there was a pause in the firing!

Another memory I have is shuffling in a long line of cadets sweeping the hillsides for unexploded ordinance.[34] I can feel the hot Okanagan breeze blowing like a blast furnace over the seared earth of Mission Hill. I can smell the lavender-sweet aroma of the sage brush. I remember picking the burrs out of the woollen puttees[35] that we wrapped around our ankles. And I can feel my skin prickling with the fear of encountering rattlesnakes, knowing that these hills were full of them and that not so long before, a boarder at Vernon Prep School had been killed by a coiled rattler. I can still hear the clack-clack-clack of the chirping crickets, too similar to the sounds of a rattlesnake. Would it be better to lose a leg to a rusty mortar shell, or die from the bite of a cranky rattlesnake?

During our six weeks at Vernon, each company of cadets was trucked some twenty miles up the road towards Kamloops to the army range at Glen Emma, to participate in a three-day "scheme." At Glen Emma we lived and slept in the bush, with our meals prepared in army mobile kitchens. The first thing my platoon had to do when we arrived was dig a latrine for the whole company. I guess building a latrine

---

[34] Since that time I have learned that hikers have been killed by stumbling across these dud shells on the hills in the Army Camp.

[35] Ankle protectors, like gaiters, made of 3 inch-wide strips of wool cloth, a yard or so long, that are wrapped around the lower shins and boot-tops.

before doing anything else is an army thing, because it was the first thing that Dad did when he took our family camping.

Each day at Glen Emma we participated in manoeuvres, at platoon and company strength, ranging back and forth across the bunch-grassed hills and bushy valleys in mock battles against one another. Each cadet was given two rounds of blank ammunition per day, and nothing could be more fun (or more dangerous) to a teenage kid than to run around all day with a real rifle and live ammunition Nothing, that is, except a real Bren gun and 30 rounds of ammunition. I was designated our platoon's Bren gunner, and quickly dispelled a well-known myth of war that recruits are reluctant to pull the trigger in their first fire-fight. For, at the commencement of a two-hour battle, I managed to fire off both magazines in my Bren in about ten seconds flat.

Any unused ammunition was supposed to be turned in to the quartermaster at the end of each day. But one evening some smart ass turned his unused ammunition in to the campfire. This caused a big stir, and we were all immediately assembled to be given, for the umpteenth time, the lecture about the lethal potential of blank ammunition, which can cause fatal injury at close range. Following which, we were each given two more rounds and sent out on a night exercise.

During that particular night exercise, Doug Schneider and I found ourselves cut off from our platoon. We were on a reconnaissance mission, but we became lost and we spooked a herd of horses, which panicked and crashed through a barbed-wire fence. The resulting chaos and commotion blew our cover and we soon began to hear sounds of long grass swishing against legs in the darkness nearby. We pressed ourselves into the ground and whispered together about our plight. It was very scary knowing that a couple of dozen rounds of live blank ammunition were aimed at us in total darkness by a bunch of idiots who had no hesitation about throwing bullets into campfires. Realizing that we were completely surrounded, and that escape was impossible, I was terrified. For some reason that I still don't understand, we

Charlie Company Rehearsing for the Searchlight Tattoo
This "gigantic spectacle" was the highlight of the Vernon cadet camp
(The *Vernon News*, August 6, 1956)

suddenly jumped up and in shaky voices demanded to the darkness that they all surrender! As our eyes focused in the gloom, we could make out the ghostly shapes of a dozen horses looking up from their grazing and staring at us in disbelief.

The highlight of Vernon cadet camp was the Searchlight Tattoo. It was a one-night spectacle put on by the army cadets in the hills above Kalamalka Lake. By all accounts it was a fantastic show. The *Vernon News* called it a "gigantic spectacle of lights, colourful bands, simulated warfare, the precision of marching men, all set against a background of trees and rolling hills." Eight-hundred cadets staged this remarkable performance to an audience of 12,000 people seated in a light rainfall in the surrounding hills. (A staggering number, since the entire population of Vernon at that time was less than 9,000 people!)[36]

---

[36] In the audience that night was an eight-year-old Vernon girl, Sandra Otway, whom I would meet eleven years later, and marry in 1969.

167

The event that night commenced with a re-enactment of the landing of Bonnie Prince Charlie in 1745 to reclaim the throne of England from George II's House of Hanover. It was a memorable scene, with a burning cross in the Okanagan darkness and the thin, lonely call of the bagpipes beckoning the clans to gather, their colourful tartans picked out by the roving searchlights as they emerged from the hills.

The marching bands included the Royal Canadian Engineers in their scarlet dress uniforms and the kilted MacIntosh Girls Pipe Band from Vernon. The army displayed its development from earliest times with a pageant of infantry uniforms through the ages, starting with a demonstration of the Roman legions using their shields as an armoured wall in their famous tortoise formations. The audience was enthralled by a flame-throwing demonstration, and jeep and field-gun assembly competitions involving the camps' driver-mechanic cadets and a team of navy cadets. And the simulated atomic bomb blast, with its spectacular mushroom shaped cloud was a stark reminder of the realities of the Cold War.

My own part in this grand theatre was a re-enactment of the Battle of Cutknife Creek, which occurred at Battleford, Saskatchewan, during the second Louis Riel Uprising, in 1885. I was a rifleman in the Queen's Own Rifles, and for two weeks we had practised our roles every day and a couple of nights (to acclimatize to the darkened terrain). We wore period uniforms (current army issue, but dyed green), carried long flintlock rifles fitted with bayonets, and we marched at double-time. Formed up in two ranks, with the front row kneeling and the back standing, we learned to fire our rifles and change places while reloading. Our enemy was Chief Poundmaker and his Cree Indians, naturally played by our native campmates from the prairies (including Peter Big Head, Alan Wolf Leg, and Lawrence Pantherbone from my own Charlie Company). Clad in loin cloths and wielding hatchets and clubs, their intensity showed a little too much purpose and glee, as though they were trying to rewrite the outcome of that one-sided battle. Unfortunately I didn't get to experience the thrill of victory, for it was written into the script that I was killed early in the battle (a hatchet blow by my buddy Pantherbone) and carried from the battle ground in, of all things, an ambulance actually drawn by a real horse.

By the time our seven weeks were up, I was sorry to leave. The entire experience had been an adventure, and overcoming the challenges was so rewarding. To quote the *Vernon News*, ". . . the young soldiers were . . . a fine bunch of lads willing to forego the summer pursuits of their schoolmates in order to equip themselves a little more substantially for adult life." It was as though I had passed into manhood.

Except for that puberty thing.

Reluctant Pair of Swingers
Donald and me sitting out yet another dance

Chapter 18

Girls and Romance

No biography would be complete without a little love and romance.

Except mine. I never got over my awkwardness around girls.

And no wonder. What girl would be interested in a scrawny little geek who skulked through the woods tracking animals and building bivouacs? While my classmates were charming the ladies, I was clomping through the marshes in gum boots, hunting for birds or trapping muskrats.

And besides, I had other interests; I was too busy playing sports. When I wasn't shooting rats or fishing for smelts, my daylight hours were filled with kicking, throwing and hitting balls. And my evenings were devoted to Latin and history and poetry. Any hours left over were crammed with household chores like mowing the lawn or raking leaves. No time for girl germs.

Don't misunderstand me. I valued girls. Elsie and Patience could climb trees with the best of us, and there was a girl in my Pasley Island summers who could put a spiral on a football as well as any guy. Like all boys, I also had my teenage crushes. Each summer at Pasley my young heart ached with secret love for the older and unattainable teenage girls who sang "Clementine" and "On Top of Old Smokey" in the shadows around Pasley evening bonfires.

I knew my limitations. I was invisible around girls. By the time I was fourteen, the pencil lines on the cupboard door that marked my growth barely recorded a height of 5 ft 3 in; and I weighed less than 100 pounds. My classmates called me Runt. And sometimes they called me Pixie. In Grade 10, even the school doctor called me a runt. I remember one examination in Dr Stoffman's office in Kerrisdale when his exact words were "What a measly specimen you are!" No wonder the girls didn't notice me.

To build up my body, Dr Stoffman instructed my parents that I should drink half a bottle of Guinness a day. I don't know if the Guinness increased my stature, but my drinking it sure impressed my school chums.

The age of puberty came late for me. In my high school years my pre-pubescence was hard to disguise. Each day when I showered after sports I felt the eyes of the whole senior school on my under-developed private parts. Even in Grade 11, I draped a towel strategically in front of me as I walked the gauntlet of hairy adolescents changing from their rugby strip.

Eight years at an all-boys school only widened the gulf between me and girls in dresses. The most painful memories of my childhood involve dancing. Together, with the rest of my Grade 10 class, I took dancing lessons at York House School. But I never got the hang of it. I was always out of time with the music or stepping on my partner's toes. And I dreaded the ordeal of making small-talk with my partner. I felt inferior to girls, and I hated the intimacy of slow waltzes at school dances.

Even more, I detested the modern music — rock and roll. Watching the *Ed Sullivan Show* with my parents on a Sunday evening in September 1956, I saw Elvis Presley for the first time. My parents were shocked by his greasy bad-boy hair and gyrating hips. Everyone called him Elvis the Pelvis. "More like Enis the Penis," said my dad. I couldn't admit it to my friends, but I shared my parents' distaste for the new rock and roll. That same month, not far from our house, Little Richard played at the Kerrisdale Arena, as Bill Haley and the Comets had done earlier that summer, and needless to say I boycotted both performances.

Elvis on Television
I detested Rock 'n' Roll. Elvis only reminded me of
my shortcomings with girls

By Grade 11, many of my classmates had girlfriends. In those days the in-crowd had boyfriend-girlfriend relationships and teenagers paired off in couples for evenings and social activities. A typical weekend date would be an evening at the movies followed by a Triple-O burger at the White Spot drive-in. The real swingers would borrow their parents' car and finish the evening with fogged-up windows, parked at the Simon Fraser monument on S.W. Marine Drive, near the mouth of the river. Imagine how they would have teased me, had they known that my weekends were also spent near the Simon Fraser monument — but trapping rodents instead!

My brother didn't have any trouble with the girl thing. He was always going out on dates. Girls even asked *him* out! He kept a list of excuses in a drawer beside our telephone in case the wrong girl called: "Sorry, family dinner that night." "Too bad, dentist appointment that afternoon." "Doctor says I've got chicken pox."

But not me. I was so hopeless in the girl department that years later, in my final year of Engineering at UBC — and this is the honest truth — my classmate Bill Crawford (who played tackle for the NFL New York *Giants*) told everyone that "Bob Ross is the only guy in town that a girl can go out with and *regain* her virginity!"

A Proud Moment
Finally, having finished high-school and no longer a runt,
I'm escorting a pretty girl to her school dance.

In those days, sex was a big secret. Sex scenes in movies were pretty tame — fully clothed and no prolonged kisses. According to Hollywood, even married couples slept in separate beds. Until I left high school, the closest I ever got to seeing a female breast was a black and white photo of a Zulu maiden in a dog-eared copy of one of Uncle Harry's old *National Geographic* magazines.

It wasn't until Grade 11 that I actually went on a date with a girl. A Crofton House girl, whom I'd never met, asked me for a blind date to her school dance. Mum drove me to her house. Standing at her door, gripping in my sweating hands the cardboard box containing her corsage, a white gardenia, was one of the most painful moments of my life. As I contemplated the choice between ringing the doorbell and committing suicide, the door opened to reveal an equally nervous young lady with a face full of pimples and a mouthful of orthodontics. She turned out to be a sweet girl and the evening was bearable. Thankfully she led the dances, let me walk all over her feet, and didn't insist that we talk.

I managed to avoid the pain of further school dances and blind dates until the occasion of my graduation. For our grad dance we all handed the school secretary the name of the girl we wished to invite; and engraved invitations were sent out by the school. Three weeks later, at morning assembly, The Beak announced to the whole world that two girls had not replied to these formal invitations. What kind of girl, The Beak asked, could be so uncouth?

He read out the names. It was my final failure at schoolboy romance.

Canoe Builders — October 1957
This canoe that Donald and I built would provide
our final childhood adventures together

Chapter 19

Voyageurs of the Lower Fraser

Whenever Donald and I looked for adventure during our last couple of years of high school, we found it on the Fraser River. Throughout our childhood we had spent countless days sneaking along the river's foreshore, hunting birds along its banks and trapping muskrats in its marshes. Constrained by the water's edge, we began to dream of ways to escape the land and enter the excitement of the river itself.

As we grew older, the river traffic caught more of our attention — fish boats, freighters, and tugs with strange tows. There was much more boat traffic in the 1950s, and each passing ship had its own mystique and its own story to tell. Coastal freighters and supply ships chugged down the river, on their way to logging and fishing camps that have long since closed down. Pile-drivers, work boats, sawdust and gravel scows, dredges and a host of other shipping serving isolated communities that in those days couldn't be reached by road or by air.

Watching the coming and going of the boats, we fantasized about their world of adventure. The timber-cruisers coming home from surveying trees in foggy northern inlets, returning to shipyards that no longer exist, like the Celtic Shipyards at the foot of Balaclava Street. When fishing was in season, we'd recognize seiners, trollers and gillnetters, laden with salmon and herring, heading for canneries that have since disappeared. Occasionally we'd spot one of the dwindling fleet of whaling boats leaving the BC Packers' wharves for the last of the whale harvests.[37]

To enter this fascinating world on the river, Donald and I decided to build ourselves a canoe. Once the decision was made, we worked like fiends and, less than six weeks later, at the end of November 1957, we were paddling down the Fraser River on our maiden voyage.

We found plans for building a 16-foot open Canadian canoe in a 1919 publication of *The Boy Mechanic*, a how-to book which had been lying around my home all through my childhood. It had entertained my father when he was a kid. Its 500 pages boasted "800 things for boys to do," from how to construct a boy's motor car or a steam-propelled motorcycle to making a trap for coyotes or "using a feather as an x-ray lens." With no TV to entertain us on rainy days, we turned to books like *The Boy Mechanic* to find projects and activities. The pages on building a canoe had often caught my attention, and finally I was going to build it.

It wasn't customary in those days for kids to involve their parents in activities of this kind. Donald and I seldom consulted our fathers on other projects, so we didn't expect any help or advice on this one. Anyway, building and fixing things wasn't one of my dad's skills. For a workshop, we took over the unused woodshed behind the old cottage at the end of our garden. An elderly couple had lived in this cottage during the War and its woodshed was still littered with hog-fuel and sacks of sawdust that brought back decade-old memories of the winter warmth in the cottage, the huge cast iron woodstove with its sawdust hopper and hot-water reservoir and the delicious smells of fresh baking.

But this was autumn, and the evenings were short and there was no warmth in the woodshed. We worked long shivering hours by lamp

---

[37] Humpbacks were harvested off the BC coast until ten years later. 15 were killed in the last year, 1967.

light in the shed and, by the end of October, the framework, the ribs and thwarts were all complete. We bent the ribs and the stems by boiling them in a large round laundry tub balanced over a bonfire beside the woodshed. I have a vivid memory of progress being temporarily interrupted one morning when the laundry tub slipped and badly scalded my foot. However this set-back didn't stop production.

The canoe was sheathed in cedar planking, which had to be carefully selected for straight, knot-free grain. At the Reliance Lumber yard on East Hastings Street we found a 20-foot length of cedar 3" x 8", straight-grained without a single knot or blemish for its entire length. It would be impossible to find a straight-grained clear piece of cedar like that today — and we only paid nine dollars! We strapped the wood to the roof of our '49 Plymouth and took it to a cabinetmaker on West Boulevard, to be sliced into 1/8th-inch-thick planks, which Donald then carried home. Only Donald would have had the strength to perform such a feat — walking eight blocks carrying a bunch of twenty foot planks on his shoulder, their ends sagging to the ground in front and behind!

We attached the planking to the ribs with tiny brass screws — some 700 of them, just ¼-inch long. Within a week we had bought out the entire stock of these little screws from every hardware store on the west side of town. By the time we'd canvassed the hull, varnished it and covered it with a couple of coats of blue paint, we'd each put in over a hundred hours. That's a staggering 2½ hours each, every day for five weeks! The canoe's final cost was $78.05.[38]

On November 24, as the great V's of geese passed overhead on their southward migration, we launched our beautiful craft in the North Arm booming grounds on the Fraser River. We portaged from S.W. Marine Drive down through the woods to the bottom of the ravine where we had spent the previous winter snaring muskrats.

High on the bluff directly above our launch site was the highway look-out with its monument commemorating Simon Fraser's voyage

---

[38] Details recorded in my Oct/Nov 1957 journal entries.

of discovery in 1808. I loved the symbolism — our start as voyageurs, as couriers-des-bois, was the exact point where the great explorer had ended his canoe trip down the river that bears his name, precisely 150 years before! (While I knew from my Grade 8 history class a little about the voyageurs and Simon Fraser's discovery, it wasn't until later that I learned the circumstances around Simon's hasty retreat, in fear that he and his party were about to be attacked by the treacherous Musqueams. The same Musqueams whose twelve-year-old descendents had chased Donald and me off their reserve, threatening to scalp us with their scissors, a couple of years before).

The journal which I kept at the time shows that by the end of December, Donald and I had already paddled our new canoe in the mouth of the Fraser eight times. Where did we find the time? We were in the midst of Christmas exams in our graduation year, and no one spent more hours cramming for end-of-term exams than me!

We'd carry the canoe, slipping and sliding down the steep winter path toward the shacks which housed the men who worked on the log booms. If the tide was up we could drop the boat in the water and glide through the leads between the booms to the open river. But sometimes we'd have to portage over the booms, a process made much easier by our log-hopping experiences from previous winters.

I loved paddling the canoe in the Fraser. Its currents were never idle. The relentless flow kept us in continuous motion, on a never-ending ride. The river would sweep us toward pilings and log booms and hidden dangers like shoals and water-logged deadheads. If we dropped our guard, the current could drive us against a log boom, capsize the canoe, and suck us down to drown beneath the logs. There was a special thrill in being borne along by the ebbing tide, steering within inches of some stationary piling or fixture, and then digging in your paddle for a hair's breath miss as you shot past.

Our top paddling speed was only five miles an hour, which wasn't always enough to match the river's flow. The combination of the river's current and an ebbing tide often made upstream travel impossible without the assistance of friendly eddies and backwaters.

Paddling was slow, but nonetheless quick enough to avoid the river traffic. We were on constant alert for the approach of bigger ships which appeared out of nowhere, slicing past at high speed. And we kept our distance from the little boom-boats as they darted about, assembling logs into booms.

I also marvelled at how noiselessly we could paddle. Our canvas-covered hull enabled remarkable stealth as it slipped quietly through the water. We'd delight in seeing how close we could sneak up, unobserved, drifting without sound toward creatures such as herons standing like statues on logs, and watch them suddenly take flight with startled squawks.

Donald and I settled into paddling with determination. I always handled the stern paddle, the position that steers and enjoys the fun of controlling the boat. I learned to feather my blade at the end of each stroke, applying an instant of sideways pressure to turn us to port or starboard. Keeping the boat in a perfectly straight line became a passion for me (like my obsession in cadets for marching in perfect line and column). I'd sight along Donald's head to a distant point on the shoreline, and focus on holding that line, frequently peeking over my shoulder to ensure that our wake left no tell-tale zigs or zags.

Donald's strength and endurance were needed in the bow. It was a combination that worked well. We developed a rhythm and could comfortably keep up a rate of over 30 strokes per minute for hour after hour if necessary, which it often was when fighting upwind against river and tide in the estuary. As we gained experience, our paddles became synchronized without effort and we learned to complement each other's strokes without discussion.

Iona Island became a frequent destination. Those were the days when it really was an island, before it became home to the region's sewage treatment plant. There was no outfall jetty or connection to Sea Island. We'd light a driftwood fire in the Iona sand dunes and cook a meal before exploring and beach combing. We shared the island with its only inhabitant, an eccentric old hermit who lived in a draughty, weather-beaten driftwood shack. I remember his wire-rimmed glasses with the cracked lenses, repaired with scotch tape that was yellowed and peeling away. He fascinated us with tales of "the good old days" when clouds of migrating geese would darken the skies and the river mouth was boiling with herring, so thick they could be scooped up with a rake.

We discovered for ourselves the huge flocks of snow geese visiting the river estuary to rest on their southward winter journey. That month the marshes were sometimes white as snow, as the geese in their thousands gathered at the shore. Their constant cackling and calling to their incoming friends was a wonderful, stirring sound. And amongst the log booms we often found wounded ducks — mallard and widgeon and teal — their wings broken by bird-shot from the hunters' guns. We chased them down with our canoe, cornering the most feeble and wringing their necks to put them out of their misery. Sometimes they would dive and grasp the reed stems in their bills, holding themselves under water for several minutes, fighting to save their bird-shot doomed lives. We marvelled at their courage and tenacity.

My favourite outings that winter on the river were the foggy days. Vancouver used to get many more days of fog every year and it was much thicker than any fog we get now. It resulted from the airborne particles given off by the coal-, wood- and sawdust-burning furnaces in homes and industry, and the beehive burners at the sawmills — there must have been twenty sawmills along the North Arm of the Fraser alone. The air would be very still and the fog would be white and solid and thick. So thick that I could barely see beyond Donald in the bow of the canoe.

The heavy stillness of the fog was palpable, other-worldly. In the silence, sounds were distinct but muffled. I remember the sounds of the unseen water-birds — the shrill cry of the Western Grebes, the whistle of the beating wings of a passing flight of goldeneyes, somewhere above the fog. I remember sitting quietly in the motionless canoe, lying dead in the water with our paddles idle, and the shock and surprise as a buoy or a wooden piling broke through the curtain of white, without warning, and revealed how fast we were being carried by the current.

The eerie blasts of unseen fog horns pierced through the gloom all around. It was impossible to figure out their distance. It was confusing because the next time you heard them they seemed to come from a different direction. The tide or current may have been turning the canoe, but you didn't know it because the fog obscured any reference points.

Suddenly you'd hear the deep-throated throb of powerful engines pounding down on you. You were in imminent danger and in the stillness you could hear your heart beat. All of a sudden, a ghostly shape — and the white fog-curtain was ripped open by the charging prow of a monstrous ship!

In that instant I'd have a flash of Huckleberry Finn's adventure while rafting down the Mississippi in heavy fog, the night when they had to dive overboard as a big paddle-wheeler ran right over them. That's when all those hours of team work on the paddles really paid off. No time to jump overboard. No time to talk about it — bow paddle digs in, stern paddle backwaters, and we'd slide off with inches to spare, riding the curling bow wave down the length of the monstrous hull as it glided back into the soup, the curtain closing behind it as suddenly as it had opened.

Those were the biggest thrills on the river!

Into the Unknown
Johnny dropped Donald and me off at the edge of civilization

Chapter 20

Into the Wild

Many of my childhood fantasies were nourished by the map on my bedroom wall. Above the desk in my room hung a large topographic rendering of British Columbia, a beautiful portrayal of the province published by the Vancouver *Province* newspaper, which showed in colourful hues and shades the rivers and lakes, the glaciers and mountains. Often, while poring over my school homework, I'd gaze up at the map and find myself exploring some wilderness valley. I'd trace with my finger every river in our vast province from its source in the white of the high glaciers, twisting through the brown and the green to its final ocean destination.

I'd wondered about the river that flowed from the remote Pemberton Valley into the top of Harrison Lake, only a couple of hours drive from Vancouver. It was called the Lilloett River. Could this be a river trip for our new canoe? Perhaps Donald and I could catch the train to Pemberton, and put our canoe into the Lilloett River and drift down to Harrison Lake, where maybe we'd be able to hitch a ride back to civilization on a logging camp supply boat.

I proposed the idea of a canoe trip to Donald for the Easter week in the spring of 1958. It would be the last opportunity for the two of us to share a wilderness experience. Two months later we would graduate from high school and start divergent college and career paths. We needed to celebrate the end of our boyhood alliance with one last adventure.

During our cycling trip the previous Easter break, in 1957, Donald and I had spent four rain-soaked days camping without a tent on Vancouver Island, and we figured that if we could survive that, we could handle any wilderness outing. It looked like canoeing down the Lilloett would be the perfect trip for us.

Our plans were well under way before we told our parents. By this point in our lives, we pretty much made our own decisions and didn't expect our parents to object. My mum and dad, whose interest in our new canoe hadn't even extended as far as observing whether it actually floated, simply nodded their heads in agreement. After all, they'd observed during the eight summers that our family had spent together on Pasley Island that I could handle rowboats and driftwood rafts. But Donald's dad was worried enough to make enquiries about the river. He discovered from the BC Forest Service that for some of its length the Lilloett is a wild torrent with serious rapids and steep canyons, which at that time (before the introduction of fibreglass kayaks) would have been considered impossible for canoes. Donald's dad talked us into choosing a different river. I was very disappointed, but knowing what I now know, some fifty years later, I realize that Dr Williams probably saved our lives.

But no problem. The map on my wall showed other long narrow lakes wedged between the mountains. One that might be promising was Pitt Lake. The far end of Pitt Lake was pretty remote, and a neat thing about it was that we might be able to return to Vancouver by paddling down into the Fraser and all the way to the very foot of Macdonald Street. The end of our canoe adventure wouldn't even require someone to pick us up.

Pitt Lake in those days was remote. It was not accessible by road. Somewhere in the hills above Pitt Lake there was rumoured to be a lost gold mine. Uncle Phil told me once that he'd grubstaked a prospector who said he knew where the mine was, but the guy vanished into the woods and never showed up again. Perhaps Donald and I might get lucky.

On the day before Good Friday, my brother drove us in our '49 Plymouth up the Fraser Valley to the river which flows from Pitt Lake. It was a long drive from Vancouver, along the Lougheed Highway through Burnaby, past the stately grounds of Essondale — the huge asylum which housed thousands of mentally ill, and on through Coquitlam to the Pitt River. Back then, there was none of today's urban sprawl; civilization pretty well ended at Port Moody and New Westminster. There were only fields and forests where today are the shopping malls and industrial parks and massive sub-divisions of Coquitlam.

Johnny dropped us where a bridge carried the Lougheed Highway over the Pitt River. We loaded our stuff into the canoe and started paddling north, upriver towards the mountains with a week's supply of grub. Our food fitted neatly into a wooden butter box (which was a remarkably compact larder, considering frozen and freeze-dried foods weren't yet available).

To appease our parents we took along a couple of life jackets. They made good pillows or comfy seats, but we never wore them.

By mid-afternoon we had paddled a dozen miles. We rounded the point where the river flows out of Pitt Lake, and the first of the mountain ridges quickly closed in behind us. We made camp before nightfall on a beach in a sheltered little bay three or four miles up the west side of the lake. As we sat by our campfire in the evening glow of a full moon, looking out toward the northern wilderness, I was really excited. We'd paddled almost fifteen miles and set up camp without difficulty. For supper we'd fried up the trout that Donald caught on his split bamboo rod with its silk-wrapped ferrules (using a fly that he'd tied himself). This trip was settling in to be a great adventure.

But later, as we lay in our sleeping bags on the gravel beach, we were awakened by an animal rustling through our food box. In the darkness we could neither see the intruder nor scare it away. Perhaps

1958 Canoe Trip
imposed on 1987 satellite image

Vancouver

Home on Macdonald Street

ⓧ

Ⓕ FINISH

Iona Island

Sea Island

Canoe dumped in log jam
SECOND & THIRD NIGHTS
Pitt Lake
FIRST NIGHT
FOURTH & LAST NIGHTS
Lower Pitt River
START
Lougheed Highway
New Westminster
Patullo Bridge
Fraser River

it was only a mouse or a pack-rat, but in the stillness of the night it sounded like a grizzly bear. We secured the food between our sleeping bags, but the incident — the first encounter of this trip with a wild animal — unsettled me.

Off in the distant woods I heard the cry of some unidentified creature — a blood-chilling sound like a woman screaming, which years later I learned was the cry of a cougar. I began to feel very alone. I recalled my favourite lines from Robert Service's "The Shooting of Dan McGrew":

> *Were you ever out in the Great Alone,*
> *when the moon was awful clear,*
> *And the icy mountains hemmed you in*
> *with a silence you most could hear;*
> *With only the howl of a timber wolf,*
> *and you camped there in the cold,*
> *A half-dead thing in a stark dead world,*
> *clean mad for the muck called gold;*

As I lay on my back staring up at the star-covered sky, the endlessness of the black void unnerved me. I scanned the heavens, searching for the pinpoint track of America's first-ever satellite which had just been launched into orbit. A couple of months earlier I had managed to spot the two Russian *Sputniks*, both of which were launched while we were building our canoe last fall. My mind kept replaying the same old Cold War worries of Russian missiles and long lines of refugees evacuating a vaporized Vancouver. Oh well, I thought, at least we are safe from the bombs this week. Here beyond the mountains, complete with canoe and camping gear, we could start a new life in the wilderness.

But I couldn't get back to sleep. Today's travel had taken us beyond the security of the familiar world. All my life I'd grown accustomed to the wall of mountains along the north side of the Fraser Valley and seeing them as the edge of my world, the very cusp of civilization.

The Great Alone
Beyond Vancouver's mountainous skyline, Pitt Lake was remote and unexplored

I knew from years of gazing at the map in my bedroom just how rugged and remote was British Columbia on the other side of Vancouver's mountainous skyline. It was as though the mountains were a screen, like a painted theatre set, a two dimensional barrier holding back the unknown. And today we had penetrated that screen, into the uncharted and unexplored. Perhaps I was overwhelmed by the Great Alone, for I felt a great loneliness.

The next morning, after a hearty breakfast of bacon and eggs, we set off again up the lake. As we paddled, I shared my apprehension with Donald. We recalled the misery of camping in the rain the previous Easter, when, discouraged and dispirited, we abandoned our campsite in the gloom of Cathedral Grove and relocated to the beach at Cameron Lake. Perhaps it was simply homesickness on the first night away from family and friends. Even Tom Sawyer and Huck Finn felt homesick their first night on the Mississippi when they and Joe Harper ran away to become pirates.

We stopped for lunch at a big water fall, and fished and paddled on lazily, until we reached the far end of the lake in mid afternoon. The Upper Pitt River flows into the north end of Pitt Lake, and we paddled up it for a mile or so, looking for a suitable campsite clear of the forest darkness.

After scouting out one potential site, we returned to the river's edge — to see our canoe drifting away in the current, already fifty yards downstream! All our possessions were disappearing around the bend in the river — axe, knives, compass, sleeping bags, food for a week, cooking pots, survival kit, fishing gear, bows and arrows. Losing the canoe was one thing, but survival in April without any provisions, or even the most elementary equipment, would have been a disaster.

It is difficult today to visualize how isolated and remote was the back country in the 1950s. There were no cottages anywhere along the shores of Pitt Lake. There was a little logging further north, but the lake saw virtually no recreational use. There were no cell phones to call for help, nor global-positioning systems to tell you where you were. The wilderness of British Columbia was less traveled than almost anywhere in the world. Civilization nibbled at the edges of the forests but seldom penetrated more than a hundred yards beyond the high-ways. And no paved road crossed the province from east to west or north to south. In fact, from where we stood at that moment, watching our canoe disappear, it was possible to walk all the way to the North Pole without crossing even one paved road! Sure, float planes could land on the lakes, but there was no simple way to access the primeval forest. Roads of any type were scarce, and four-wheel drive vehicles scarcer. There were no snowmobiles for winter access. There were virtually no helicopters to find or rescue you. The only penetration of this wilderness was by canoe.

And we'd just lost ours!

We ran through the forest in desperate pursuit of our disappearing lifeline, but at the next clearing we saw that the current was carrying it away faster than we could thrash through the heavy undergrowth. If our canoe was to snag on one of the many sweepers which trailed into the water from the undercut banks, the current would flip it in an instant and dump our supplies to the mercy of the river. Without hesitation Donald dove into the current and swam for our very survival.

It was a tense race, with the current sucking them both toward dangerous sweepers — tree branches waiting to entangle whatever swept by. Catching up to the boat was hard enough for Donald, but keeping it upright and wrestling it to the shore took all his skill. I ran downstream through the woods to intercept them at a bend in the river. As he struggled in the ice-cold water, fighting the current and slippery footing, Donald managed to get a rope to me, and our boat and supplies were saved.

That evening we built a huge campfire to dry Donald's clothes and to raise our spirits. We made a rice pudding to warm our stomachs, and we lay in our sleeping bags beneath the canoe to escape the first rainfall of the trip. No homesickness that night — just tired relief and thankfulness.

Morning on the third day dawned clear and cold. It was windy and there was not much warmth to the sun. After a breakfast of pancakes, we packed up the makings of a lunch and started up river, leaving all our gear in the campsite. We paddled upstream, working the back-eddies and slower water on the insides of the river bends. After an hour of hard paddling, the current became too strong for us to make headway. It was time to track the canoe from the river bank.

Tracking a canoe was something I'd recently read about in a book by R.M. Patterson, called *The Dangerous River*. In 1928 Patterson had wintered up the remote Nahanni River in the North West Territories, and his book was a gripping tale of his adventures on the river. He described a method of walking alongside the fast stretches of river, holding the canoe out in the current by means of a long line with one end attached to the bow and the other to the rear seat. By pulling on one end or the other of the rope, you could manoeuvre the canoe back or forth in the current, steering it around obstacles as you walked up river. The technique proved to be surprisingly simple; we found that it

Tracking the Canoe
*Rehearsing for the fast stretches of water we would
soon encounter on the Upper Pitt River*

was effortless to drag the canoe up the riffles and faster stretches of river at a speed that was limited only by the pace that we could walk.

After an hour or so of easy tracking, we encountered a large log jam. Hundreds of logs of all sizes were jammed against the banks on both sides of the river, leaving a narrow gap at the middle where the current raced through in a wildly tumbling chute. The current was way too fast to paddle against, and the jumble of logs made tracking impossible from either bank.

So we jumped into the canoe and tried to pull our way up the chute, hand over hand, grabbing the ends of the logs, and inching our way upstream. The current was so strong and the logs so unstable that we kept slipping backwards and losing any ground we had gained.

After about twenty minutes of back-aching struggle, a log suddenly dislodged and our canoe was pinned by the force of the water against the top of the log jam. Like true couriers-des-bois, we weren't wearing life jackets. Soaked and scared, Donald and I managed to scramble to safety across the log jam. Somehow the canoe extricated itself and went shooting off down the river.

We'd been in the wilderness for only two days, and already we'd lost our canoe twice!

I watched in horror as the smooth blue hull floated away. It was upside down. Momentarily forgetting our predicament, I caught myself admiring its smooth shape and deep blue colour. I thought what a shame — after all those hours of sanding and bending and steaming and clamping and tightening hundreds of tiny screws in the woodshed at the back of our yard. For a moment I forgot that this was our lifeline to civilization. For a moment I forgot that an upside down canoe is an empty canoe. And an empty canoe means no survival gear.

Once again Donald swam after it, braving the freezing water to retrieve it a short way downstream. Fortunately only the spare paddle and life jackets were lost — everything else was in a pack lashed to a thwart, saved but soaking. Good thing we'd left most of our possessions back at camp! We tried to light a fire but the matches were ruined, so we just spread our wet clothes on a gravel bar and warmed up by running around naked in the weak sun. The bread for our lunch was soaked, so we ate our sandwiches without it.

Three hours later, our clothes had partially dried and we headed downriver to our campsite. Paddling a canoe downriver through riffles and rapids is exhilarating. If you make a wrong decision or get into trouble the river never stops to give you time to correct your error. It just washes you further into the danger, and it never relents. For the inexperienced it's like a pin-ball in a penny arcade, bouncing from rock to rock, ending with the disaster of an unforgiving boulder or sweeper upsetting the canoe.

But with skill, canoeing downstream can become the reality version of a modern video game — a stroke of the paddle, backwater here, forward there, twisting and turning around the procession of boulders and hazards that keep flying towards you. And for an experienced canoeist, reading the ripples that betray the hazards, and deftly slipping the boat through the fastest water can be pure joy. Donald and I had practised hard since our first outing last November, and letting the current carry us swiftly down the river on this afternoon was like a gift from God.

We slept well that night.

The next morning we broke camp and again rode the euphoria of the friendly current downstream, back to Pitt Lake. Then almost twenty miles of paddling on the flat water of the lake, so calm in comparison, so straight and unvarying. Dwarfed by the mountains around us, slowly but relentlessly advancing, stroke after stroke, like a tiny insect rippling the water's surface, mile after mile, hour after hour.

It was late afternoon when we finally reached the mouth of Pitt Lake and entered the river flowing from it toward the Fraser. We passed a small boat tied to the bank and noticed two figures cooking around a campfire. Pulling ashore shortly afterwards, we made camp near the mouth of a small tributary, called Widgeon Creek.

After a dinner of soup and hot dogs, we visited the nearby campers, who turned out to be two kids our own age, Ron and Errol, from New Westminster. They were the first people we'd seen during our entire adventure (but of course by now we were no longer in the lonely land beyond the mountains — we'd returned to the south side, the side of civilization).

It turned out that this was the first evening of Ron and Errol's trip and they still had fresh food. Donald and I consumed an entire loaf of their mothers' freshly baked bread with homemade raspberry jam. It sure beat our diet of sardines and carrots! We spent the evening by their fire, listening on their radio to the hockey game from Queens Park Arena, where their New Westminster *Royals* were playing my Vancouver *Canucks*. Quite a contrast to our previous evenings listening to the haunting call of the loons and the distant cries of a cougar.

Ron and Errol were on the same kind of journey as Donald and I, a final fling to honour the years of their shared youth before setting out into the world. But the difference between their style and ours was profound. They had brought along a 22-calibre rifle. We had bows and arrows! They talked about girls and Elvis Presley and fast cars. We were still making muskrat snares and riding bicycles! Their boat was a 16-foot fibreglass runabout with one of those new 25-horsepower outboard motors. We had a canoe. The difference between Ron and Errol on the one hand, and Donald and me on the other was a metaphor of the gulf between our separate boyhoods.

But we nerds got on well with the two swingers, who came from similar homes and had the same aspirations as Donald and I. We were leery of their glitz and glamour, and I was surprised how easily they accepted two misfits like us. We spent the next day with Ron and Errol, hiking to a small lake at the top of the prominent knoll between Widgeon Creek and Pitt Lake. At the little lake on the summit we found a small raft, and Donald and I fished while Ron and Errol blasted away with their gun at passing ducks. But none of us managed to bring home food for the pot.

It rained heavily all through that night. Without a tent, Donald and I dodged the downpour by sleeping under our canoe. (Ron and Errol slept soundly beneath the dry canopy of their fibreglass boat.) Dawn on our sixth day broke heavy and wet and the rain didn't look like letting up, so we decided to head for home.

Another day of ceaseless paddling. Thirty strokes to each minute, hour upon hour. Change sides every couple of minutes. Heads down, bent to the wind-driven rain. One eye open for driftwood, the other sighting over Donald's head, picking a course to a distant target. Both ears tuned to the sounds of the river, listening for danger. No respite for aching arms. No pleasure in idle chatter. No sights worth seeing along the mist-shrouded shores of the Fraser.

Soaked to the skin, we stopped only once — for lunch under the shelter of the Lougheed Highway bridge.

We paddled under the Patullo Bridge and glided past the docks of New Westminster. An eternity later, as we paddled through Marpole, a mile from home, our journey became a little easier when a tug towing a sawdust scow took pity on us. The skipper slowed as he overtook us and we managed to hitch a ride by hooking a line over a cleat on the barge. It was an exhilarating ride, surfing the scow's stern wave, teetering between overturning on its crest and being sucked beneath by it's undertow.

Finally we arrived at the foot of Macdonald Street. We turned our bow upriver and coasted to shore at our old familiar haunt, soaked and exhausted. With the help of the river's current and an ebbing tide we had paddled almost 40 miles in one day. There was nothing left but to shoulder the canoe for the mile-long portage up the Macdonald Street hill to our homes.

And so ended the last adventure of my childhood. I was three months past my seventeenth birthday. This was the final vacation of my final school year, my last holiday before I would head off to a summer job, university, a career and the world. As we portaged through the McCleery farm, the fields and sloughs where we had first experimented with the wonders of the outdoors, I saw those idyllic days of my youth pass before me.

And as my boyhood was ending, so was the old McCleery farm. This, the first non-aboriginal homestead and the last farm in Vancouver, had been bought by the City a short time before and was being converted to a golf course. I felt the nostalgia as we carried the canoe past the ditches where our little nets and jars had first scooped up frogs and tadpoles. Animal burrows in the muddy banks gave proof that at least some muskrats survived Paul's leg-hold traps. The mountain ash tree where Donald had fired his arrow through the robin's head stood alone in the field where we had often waited so patiently with our bows and arrows for the night flight of mallards. We passed the ponds which froze most winters, the outdoor ice where all the kids in our neighbourhood had learned to skate, where Donald had broken his arm in a long ago game of shinny.

We trudged up the hill past the clearing where the old McCleery farmhouse had sat for almost a hundred years. I missed the draughty old barn and ramshackle stables and chicken coops and the sheds where we'd helped the McCleery descendants with the milking and feeding and haying. Fond memories of the black and white Holstein cows heading from the fields to the barn each evening, back then a reminder that it was time to stop playing in the fields and sloughs and start home for supper up this same hill.

The canoe felt much heavier after we left the flats and began slogging up the steepest part of Macdonald Street. We used to toboggan down this hill and rocket across Marine Drive, trusting Jonathan to stop the approaching cars. In those days cars were few and far between — difficult to imagine when compared to today's unending flow of heavy university-bound traffic along Marine Drive.

The next time I peered out from under the awkward load that was biting into my shoulders we were passing Ricky Weir's home. It was from the roof of Ricky's woodshed that, in the summer of 1954, we had watched our first television. And finally the Silbernagels' huge cucumber tree, the old neighbourhood meeting place, the nerve centre of my entire childhood.

I collapsed at my front gate, exhausted from the last of the many adventures that ended in that weary but happy trudge up the Macdonald Street hill. Tired perhaps — but full of eagerness to find new fields to explore.

*Western Man is so surrounded by ideas,
so bombarded with opinions, concepts, information
structures of all sorts, that it becomes difficult
to experience anything without the intervening
filter of those structures. And the natural world
— our traditional source of direct insights —
is rapidly disappearing. Modern city-dwellers
cannot even see the stars at night. This humbling
reminder of man's place in the greater scheme
of things, which human beings once saw
every 24 hours, is denied them. It's no wonder
that people lose their bearings, that they lose track
of who they really are, and what their
lives are really about.*

— Michael Crichton, *Travels*

About the Author

Bob Ross has lived in Vancouver most of his life. He comes from a family with strong pioneer roots in British Columbia. His great grandfather Henry Cambie was sent by the Government of Canada in 1874 to survey the inlets of the west coast in order to select the terminus for the first railway across the new Dominion of Canada.

His grandfather Robert Tatlow arrived in British Columbia in 1879, where he became private secretary to the Lieutenant Governor and subsequently represented Vancouver in the provincial legislature. Tatlow was also a member of Vancouver's first Park Board and a founder of the BC Telephone Co.

Bob's Cornwall relatives homesteaded the Ashcroft Ranch in British Columbia's Cariboo in 1862. Clement Cornwall became the Lieutenant-Governor of British Columbia in 1885, and subsequently a senator in the federal government.

Bob graduated in Civil Engineering from the University of British Columbia in 1963, and served the City of Vancouver for most of his professional career as traffic engineer and streets engineer.

After retirement, Bob worked part-time for eight years in Vancouver's Downtown Eastside, on public realm projects related to that neighbourhood's current social challenges.

Bob and his wife Sandra have traveled extensively and now spend much of their time on airplanes to and from Australia and Mexico, where their two daughters are raising the grandchildren.